Deadlines
and
Datelines

ALSO BY DAN RATHER

The Palace Guard (with Gary Gates)
The Camera Never Blinks (with Mickey Herskowitz)
I Remember (with Peter Wyden)
The Camera Never Blinks Twice (with Mickey Herskowitz)
Mark Sullivan's *Our Times* (editor)

DEADLINES AND DATELINES

Dan Rather

Perennial

An Imprint of HarperCollins*Publishers*

A hardcover edition of this book was published in 1999 by William Morrow and Company, Inc.

First Perennial edition published 2000.

Library of Congress Cataloging-in-Publication Data has been applied for.

ISBN 0-688-17905-3 (pbk.)

00 01 02 03 04 RRD 10 9 8 7 6 5 4 3 2 1

FOR HUGH CUNNINGHAM,
my journalism professor
at Sam Houston State Teachers College, Huntsville, Texas,
1950–1953,
and my dear friend, 1950–present

These reports are submitted
in partial fulfillment of the continuing course
on which he launched me.

CONTENTS

Chapter 2

FOREIGN POLICIES, GLOBAL PERSPECTIVES

Chapter 3

THE WASHINGTON SCENE: POLITICS AND POLITICIANS

Chapter 4

TRIBUTES

Chapter 5

The Lighter Side

INTRODUCTION

When I'm away from my work, when I'm fishing or having dinner with my wife, someone will come up and ask, "What do you think—what do you *really* think" about the day's news in China, Russia, Washington, wherever they've seen me reporting.

Usually people are friendly, but sometimes not. Part of growing up as a reporter is learning that not everybody is going to love you and your work.

And the first part of that lesson is: almost nobody wants your opinion. People want facts, not opinions, from reporters. Ed Murrow once famously remarked that "My opinion isn't worth any more than that of the drunk at the end of the bar." And "commentary" is almost valueless—anybody can comment, whether or not they know what they're talking about. The usually taciturn Eric Sevareid was known to blow up at people who described his careful, informed, always literate news analysis as "commentary."

So when I've got time to talk for a few minutes, and the people seem friendly, I do try to make some answer. Along those lines, then, are the essays in this book. I'm no Murrow or Sevareid, but I try to avoid mere commentary and to offer solid reporting instead.

Both of the venues for which most of these essays were written share the title *Dan Rather Reporting*: my weekly newspaper column syndicated by King Features, and my daily radio program broadcast by CBS.

All of what's here was written against deadlines, often from some faraway dateline. Just before, during, or just after whatever there is to do for television, I do this writing.

Some other times I write magazine articles, work on a book project, or prepare a few remarks for a speaking engagement. Such work has a different set of deadlines, and I like it fine. But it is in the nature of my professional life that I do more writing against hard deadlines—hourly and daily—than any other kind.

Writing has never come easily to me, but I've always loved it. And I've spent a lifetime trying to make of myself a better writer. Still am trying.

Reporting may be my great passion in life, and writing helps me enjoy it more fully. I don't feel I've captured a story, really understood it, until I've sat down and written it.

The sound of my voice isn't enough—even with an anchorman's ego. Broadcasting still feels ephemeral to me. I know that the work I do for radio and television will endure—physically, anyway, so long as the tapes survive. But I can't touch the broadcast work once it's recorded. What I write is tangible. That alone makes it seem more real, more permanent.

That's why it's fair to say that, if I'd been a better speller, I probably would've spent life as a newspaperman.

That's what I started out to be. Ever since early childhood, I always wanted to be a newspaper reporter. Newspapers were exciting. Newspapers were important. Newspapers were independent and American. And newspapers were *dynamic*—as in *aero*dynamic. At least they were around our house.

My father worked with his back and his hands and his heart. He never finished high school. But he was a voracious reader of newspapers and didn't take reading lightly. If he read something he disagreed with, the newspaper flew across the living room. He was a big man with a strong arm, and that paper really traveled at an impressive velocity.

My father would throw the paper away and start shouting to my mother to telephone the subscription office; we were canceling.

He was a man of high principles and honor, my father,

which is why, having canceled a subscription, he never re-newed it. He ran through every paper in Houston, and when another paper fell out of favor, he'd go looking for the next. (There was never any question of doing without a paper.)

Eventually, he disagreed with every newspaper in the state of Texas. Which is how I developed great respect not only for newspapers but for *readers* of newspapers.

And also how mine became the only family in my Houston neighborhood to subscribe to the *St. Louis Post-Dispatch* and *The Christian Science Monitor*. We may have gotten the news a little later than other families, but we got it written the way my father liked it.

Newspapers were a habit my father would never break, and never wanted to. When he was killed in a car crash in 1962, there was a three-day-old copy of the *Monitor* in his workbag on the seat beside him.

By this time I'd already begun to work in television, which my father understood as the uncertain work I'd do until it was time for me to go back to newspapering.

I'd gotten my start in newspapers—selling them on street corners—and finally worked my way up to become a glorified stringer at the *Houston Chronicle*.

It quickly became apparent to my editors that my future lay *outside* print. It took them so long to correct my spelling errors that my stories wouldn't go to press until four or five editions had run.

I wasn't merely a poor speller, I was innovative. I could find sixteen new ways to spell "cat." I could spell "Alabama" with-out using vowels.

At last a kindly editor took me aside and, as he showed me ever so gently to the door, suggested the one word I might not have any trouble spelling: CBS.

I didn't mind. I wanted to be a writer. And CBS was known—then as now—as a writer's network. (The speller's network, of course, has always been ABC.)

Now, after long years of study and practice, and thanks to spellcheck programs on my computer, I have finally resumed my newspaper career.

I'm grateful for the challenge of turning out a weekly newspaper column. Whether some of the pieces gathered here are worthy of a book, you will judge. I'd be pleased but surprised if you liked every one of them. My hope is that you'll like at least some of them.

And if what I write winds up flying across a few American living rooms—well, it's part of an honorable tradition. I think my father would approve.

Deadlines
and
Datelines

Chapter 1

IN THE NEWS,
ACROSS AMERICA

Sometimes New York and Los Angeles seem more than a continent apart. America's cultural powerhouses are separated by so many seemingly unrelated histories, traditions, and ideas.

A surprise, then, to travel between New York and California, and discover that people on both coasts are talking about the same issue: use of violent force by police. In Los Angeles, the subject is raised by a movie, *L.A. Confidential*. In New York, the subject has been raised by a real-life case in which police officers are accused of assaulting a suspect, including alleged sexual abuse with a plunger, only to discover the suspect was innocent.

Most New Yorkers agree that the "plunger case" went way over the line. But would force have been condoned if the suspect had later been proven guilty? If he had been suspected of more serious crimes?

Such tough questions go to the heart of our desire to maintain a lawful, peaceful society. Is it possible to keep our communities safe without using some violent force? Where do we draw the line? Who decides?

Your reporter asked Dan Rosenblatt, director of the International Association of Chiefs of Police. Rosenblatt said, "What is alleged to have happened in the New York 'plunger case' is outrageous. There is and must be zero tolerance for this kind of thing among police leaders all over the country. In New York, in Los Angeles, everywhere, we're not just shaking our heads and talking about identifying and eradicating bad police. We're actively searching for ways to do it better, faster."

L.A. Confidential is fiction, of course, but it illustrates the theory that violence and corruption go hand in hand. In the film, a few L.A.P.D. officers go wrong, yet over time they develop a vast network. New Yorkers who have seen *L.A. Confidential* may rightly wonder whether the violent abuse alleged in the "plunger case" is being nipped in the bud, or allowed to grow.

This reporter spoke a few nights ago with two New York policemen as they patrolled a street dividing one of the city's wealthier neighborhoods and one of its poorest. Like the vast majority of cops across America, these were conscientious, law-abiding public servants.

One insisted the "plunger case" had to be an isolated incident. "I've never seen anything like it, never heard of anything like it, in our precinct or anywhere else. If it was widespread, we'd know."

Both cops agreed that nobody in city government or the police department, from shift supervisors to commissioners, has ever indicated in any way that anything like the violent force allegedly used in the "plunger case" would be tolerated.

"Well," said your reporter, "nobody has to *say* that it'll be tolerated. What about attitudes, signs, the mood stemming from the top?"

Lightning response: "Nothing. And I'll tell you something else. City hall administrations in this town, Democrats and Republicans, have been consistent about that. The signals, the rules have always been: be tough when you have to, but don't break the law. Every cop in this city knows: you break the law, you run a big risk. You get caught, you're going to be punished—worse than any other lawbreaker. Because you're a cop. That knowledge goes with the badge."

If they saw another cop do something illegal, would they tell? There was a stony pause.

"C'mon," your reporter said. "I've already promised not to reveal your names."

The infamous blue wall of silence came down between us, hard.

Our talk was over.

But as they left, the older one winked and said, "I did like that *L.A. Confidential*. Good flick. Liked *Donnie Brasco* better. More true to life."

Also a New York movie—not an L.A. movie. Of course.

SMALL-TOWN VALUES, BIG-TIME TRAGEDY
November 19, 1997

PEARL, MISSISSIPPI—Mayberry, North Carolina, never really existed except on television. Its biggest crime problem was Otis, the genteel town drunk—nothing the sheriff, Andy Taylor, couldn't solve armed only with a little smooth Southern talk and folksy wisdom.

Growing up in Mississippi, Tobe Ivy watched *The Andy Griffith Show* and dreamed. Dreamed of growing up to be another Sheriff Taylor, the lawman portrayed by Griffith as a gentle small-town boy turned keeper of the flame of old-fashioned virtue and values.

In his walk, talk, and kindly ways, Griffith reminded Tobe of his own father. Griffith's character was humorous. But he was also a hero to be emulated.

Today, Tobe Ivy is a police lieutenant in Pearl. He's one of two juvenile police officers here. His beat is kids. His heart aches. "And it will forever," he says gruffly.

It's been just under two months since this small Bible-Belt town was rocked by three murders—allegedly the work of teens in a satanic cult.

On October 1, Tobe Ivy got the call. Shooting at the high school. He burst into the school's "common room" to find a scene of carnage. The dead and the wounded, the bleeding and the panicked everywhere.

How and why it happened, in Pearl of all places, haunts him.

"I've long thought of our little town as a kind of 1990s version of Mayberry," he says. But Sheriff Taylor never had to deal with anything like this.

In Pearl's combined city hall and cop shop, Tobe Ivy and his colleagues believe they've solved the case. Mayor Jimmy Foster, a former police chief; Pearl's present police chief, Bill Slade; Ivy's partner, Lieutenant William "Butch" Townsend, and others have worked the clock to break the case.

A big, quiet sixteen-year-old sophomore, Luke Woodham, did the shooting, they say. He stabbed his mother to death at home, then came to school and opened fire on his classmates with a 30-30 deer rifle. Two students, including Woodham's onetime girlfriend, were killed there. Seven other students, apparently targeted at random, were wounded.

Pearl police say they've found evidence Woodham didn't act alone. They say six other teenage boys were involved. Police say these boys saw themselves as good students and socially ostracized because they didn't play on sports teams or in the award-winning school band. So they allegedly conspired to get rid of their "enemies" and win respect.

They are accused of forming a secret club called "The Kroth," a name believed taken from satanic verses. One boy, "a self-proclaimed Satanist," according to prosecutors, cast himself as "the father" of the group, with Luke Woodham as a loyal follower.

Whether any or all of this can be proved in court remains to be seen. It is a far cry from Mayberry.

Tobe doesn't look like Andy Griffith. For one thing, God didn't make him tall. He's short and stout, "just plain ol' fat, I'd call it." He shrugs. But he has Mayberry ways. His squad car is a pickup. He talks with a drawl as deep as the Delta.

He moves slowly, languidly. And his small-town values are intact after this confrontation with tragedy.

"Whatever happens in the future," Tobe Ivy says, "our Pearl will never be the same. And let me tell you something: if it can happen here, it can happen anywhere. Parents need to know that. They need to be aware, be alert, and love and hug their kids." He pauses and gets a faraway look in his eyes. "Just like folks in Mayberry did. The America of *Andy Griffith* may have been funny, people can ridicule it, but it had something we need to get back."

STILL MOVING FOR CIVIL RIGHTS
June 10, 1998

John Lewis is talking about race in America.

"We need, all of us, rededication and new inspiration to advance the cause of racial cooperation, peace, and harmony in America."

This is his story, this is his song; he has been singing it nearly all of his life long.

This night, as we talked, neither of us could know that far away, in Jasper, Texas, three white men allegedly dragged a black man to his death behind a pickup truck. We would not know of it until the next day, when news reports began to tell the story.

That story is in the present, but it is a throwback to the past, a past John Lewis and I know only too well.

We met in the very early 1960s. First in Mississippi, again in Georgia, and then in many datelines long since forgotten, as the American civil rights movement gained momentum, crested with passage of the Voting Rights Act in 1964, then crashed with the assassination of Dr. Martin Luther King, Jr., in 1968.

Lewis was a young preacher then, a Christian true-believer in nonviolence. But an extraordinarily brave one. On two occasions, this reporter saw Lewis nearly beaten to death by segregationist thugs.

In those days he was point man for numerous nonviolent civil rights campaigns. He was challenging the United States to live up to its ideals.

He still is. He believes passionately in America as a land of the free, where a diverse, multiracial mix of citizens can live the dream of liberty and justice for all.

Lewis is a United States congressman now, has been for twelve years. A Democrat from Georgia, representing a district that includes most of Atlanta.

He remains committed to an America of inclusion and universality. Like Dr. King, Lewis hopes to advance the cause of *all* Americans, working *together*.

He still believes in the dream of one America, not divided along the fault lines of race.

"But just to talk about it anymore has gone out of fashion," he says. "So many people don't want to think about, much less do anything about it." And this worries him.

In his profound and engrossing new book, *Walking with the Wind* (Simon & Schuster), he has written: "Talk is fine. Discussion is fine. But we must respond. We must act. Mother Teresa acted. She reached out to those who were left behind— the forsaken, the poorest of the poor, the sickest of the sick.

"And where did she find the strength, her focus, her fuel? She was asked that question back in 1975. Her answer was succinct. The fuel, she explained, is prayer. 'To keep a lamp burning,' she said, 'we have to keep putting oil in it.' "

That's one reason Lewis looks to America's churches and churchgoers for leadership.

Lewis is fifty-eight now, and thicker through the middle than he was when we first met. But his energy hasn't diminished. He often paces far into the night, worrying, thinking, and praying about what can be done to help America.

I picture him pacing and praying as our conversation nears an end, and he repeats the closing theme of his book.

"There is an old African proverb: 'When you pray, you move your feet.' As a nation, if we care for the Beloved Community, we must move our feet, our hands, our hearts, our resources to build and not to tear down, to reconcile and not to divide, to love and not to hate, to heal and not to kill. In the final analysis, we are one people, one family, one house— the American house, the American family."

HEALER, HEAL THYSELF, PLEASE
June 2, 1999

Most days in most ways, your average American hospital is a modern miracle.

But there are other days.

Let me tell you about a few that have come to your reporter's attention lately.

First, there's a person I've known a long time who suddenly wound up in a big-city emergency room. He'd been mugged and was beaten pretty badly.

An older, apparently very experienced X-ray operator quickly got into an argument with the younger resident physician on duty.

The older woman dominated, the younger woman cowered, the patient shuddered, and the whole scene dissolved into chaos.

Was there some kind of problem with the equipment, or with the patient himself? The patient didn't know. These health-care professionals didn't even try to explain.

Whenever the patient would say, "Will someone please tell me what the hell is going on here—and, more importantly, will someone please help me?" the answer came back every time as a version of "Just lie there and be quiet." Sometimes that answer was delivered matter-of-factly, sometimes rudely, but never politely.

After several hours, a more senior physician—or at least a more commanding one—took over. Some sense of order was restored, and the patient finally was treated.

He now calls the experience "an eye-opener."

Then there's another friend whose child suddenly became ill with excruciating internal pain.

The parents rushed the child to the nearest hospital. It happens to be one of the country's best known.

The family's experience was awful. There was a series of delays, misdiagnoses, doctors' turf wars, and open arguments among surgeons, internists, and pediatricians.

With the child's condition worsening and no sign of abatement in the doctors' squabbling, the family sought to move the child by ambulance to another hospital.

People—mostly doctors—at the first hospital sought to prevent this. And not politely so.

The parents prevailed, the child was moved, other doctors quickly diagnosed the ailment, and the child survived.

The family's reaction to their hospital troubles: "We're still astounded and angry."

Lastly, the most recent case in point: a husband's internal pain gets much worse. He awakens his wife. They call 911 and get to a hospital emergency room.

There the man lies for twelve hours—twelve hours. Doctors come and go, so do nurses. Some of the doctors conduct classes with younger doctors—over the patient. So do some of the nurses. At least that's the way it appears. Yet again, no attempt is made to explain anything to the patient or his wife.

So far as the wife could tell, nobody ever took charge. No diagnosis was made. A young doctor got into a shouting match with a lab technician—which ended with the technician cursing at the doctor and then at the astonished patient's wife.

After pleading with several hospital authorities for help, and receiving none, the wife took her husband out of the hospital and back home.

She then got him admitted to another hospital, where they were treated reasonably quickly and well.

None of these were HMO cases, which some people may find surprising.

None of these cases happened in small or rural hospitals.

These were big-time, important medical facilities, and these were patients with the means to pay for the finest care.

Now we've all heard of the stress hospital personnel face every day. Many of them aren't paid well or treated with much respect. But how many excuses can you make for this kind of behavior?

Do these cases tell us something important about possible trends in American medicine?

The answer may very well be no.

But cases like these do make you wonder.

A TRIP TO THE INNER SUBURB
May 27, 1998

EAST LOS ANGELES, CALIFORNIA—When reporters from the Northeast come to Los Angeles for the first time, they always ask to see the slums, the "inner city," the sometimes overboiling melting pot of southern California.

And when they get there, they say, "Where is it? Where are the slums?"

In truth Los Angeles doesn't have many stereotypical slums, as northeasterners understand them. Most of Los Angeles looks like a suburb: single-family dwellings, tidy yards, smallish apartment buildings. Not Simpson's Brentwood or Knots Landing, but not tenements, either.

Walk the streets of East L.A. with me. They're the living, throbbing heart of Los Angeles and, indeed, of America as it approaches the twenty-first century.

White migrants from various European heritages, from the American Midwest and South, helped build this neighborhood in the early part of this century. There followed a heavy influx of Irish and Jewish lower-and middle-class families: California dreaming, chasing the great American dream.

Today East L.A. is heavily populated by Mexicans and their American children. Your reporter finds abundant reminders that wave after wave of new immigrants from Mexico and elsewhere in Latin America have made deep, lasting changes in American culture. And in the daily life of our big cities.

You see it in Phoenix, San Antonio, and Houston. You see it in Denver, El Paso, and Miami. Each has its own booming inner city. And so do major metropoli *outside* the southern and western U.S.

Just before coming West, your reporter spent a day in New York City's thriving Spanish Harlem, and found it climbing away from the stigma "slum." New immigrants, many from Mexico, are fueling something like a boom.

But New York's Spanish Harlem is unlike the Spanish-speaking inner-city neighborhoods of the western and southern population centers. That's why northeasterners may not recognize an inner city when they see one.

"Inner suburbs," your reporter calls them. They look like suburbs. But they have the same problems—and the same potential for power—as the inner cities of the Northeast.

The center of gravity of American life has shifted in my lifetime and yours from the city to the suburb, from the Northeast to the South and West. An increasing weight within that center of gravity is immigration from Mexico, the Caribbean,

Central and South America. Its core is in neighborhoods such as East L.A.

Walking the streets of East L.A. this week, your reporter listened closely to what people are talking about, what's on their minds.

Their children and a yearning for better schools headed the list. Some still want schools to teach a majority of subjects in Spanish, but most (in this scattered, very lightweight sampling) don't. Most seem to believe that if their children don't learn English with something approaching native fluency, they will be disadvantaged for life.

That's a hot issue now. Parents, teachers, and politicians are reassessing and debating bilingual education in your state and mine. California's Proposition 227 could do away with bilingual education in that state's public schools. The results of Tuesday's vote—and, specifically, how East L.A. polled— will be scrutinized, and may wind up an important factor in your children's education.

Proposition 227 passed narrowly and is now being implemented, despite some resistance and challenges in the courts.

REGGIE DENNY
September 29, 1992

LOS ANGELES—I spent yesterday morning with Reginald Denny, his family and legal advisers, and I thought you'd like to know how he's doing.

Five months ago today, Reggie Denny was pulled from his eighteen-wheeler and brutally beaten at the intersection of

Florence and Normandie, ground zero for the L.A. riots. The beating was captured on videotape, broadcast live in Los Angeles and around the country. Some viewers realized the beating was still going on, and so rushed outside to defend Reggie. They saved his life. Even so, he was unconscious for days. He still has no memory of the beating. His injuries were severe: over one hundred fractures in his face, more than ninety of them significant.

Today, his recovery appears to have been remarkable. Reggie Denny walks with a smile on his face and a bounce in his step. If he bears a grudge against the people who beat him, this reporter couldn't detect it. Instead, Reggie Denny tries to understand the people who hurt him.

Reggie Denny is cheerful—his wit is quick and he's even willing to laugh at himself. Showing me his new pickup truck, Reggie said, "You can take the guy out of the truck, but you can't take the truck out of the guy."

Lately, Reggie has been thinking about the thoughtfulness of others. He talks about "the emotional moment when I realized that these thousands of people cared enough to write" while he was recovering. His hospital received over twenty-five thousand letters, cards, flowers, plants—and ten teddy bears. (By the way, Reggie says he got everything everybody sent, and he's sorry he hasn't finished writing all his thank-you notes.)

For a while, his eight-year-old daughter Ashley was afraid that she'd hurt him if she touched him. But Reggie marvels because, although most adults can't always express themselves, young Ashley already knows how important it is to tell him she loves him.

At a neighborhood Y.M.C.A., Ashley sometimes plays with kids who are physically challenged, on crutches or in wheelchairs. Ashley's friends were worried about Reggie. Now he gets a little choked up when he talks about it. "I'm walking around, doing okay, and they're stuck in a wheelchair—and *they're* concerned about me."

Reggie Denny says he'd like to set aside a special room in

his next house: a shrine to compassion. "I don't have an education. I don't have a Ph.D. or plaques to put on the wall. But I do have an awful lot of loving letters. And ten teddy bears. I'd like to see some guy with more than that."

LESSONS FROM A HERO
April 1, 1998

This reporter has been to Jonesboro, Arkansas, many times. It's a good town, friendly and caring, like many other towns in America.

Since March 24, Jonesboro has also been a grieving town.

Two boys are accused of a gun attack at their middle school, where four students and a teacher, Mrs. Wright, died. According to eyewitness testimony and police reports, Mrs. Wright threw herself directly in the line of fire when one of the shooters aimed at a girl student. That girl was spared: Shannon Wright was not.

In Jonesboro, as in any community touched by tragedy, the questions abound. Many of them will never be answered to anyone's satisfaction.

How did this happen? Who is responsible? What, if anything, could have been done to prevent it?

And what can we do to pay our respects to the dead?

This reporter has been thinking about that last question in particular, ever since the shootings. And I have one suggestion:

Build a monument to Shannon Wright. Not as a casualty to violence—but as a teacher. Not as a victim—but as a hero.

She deserves it.

According to friends and relatives, Shannon Wright was born to teach. When she was a little girl, she used to play teacher, giving "homework assignments" to her friends. In the

Jonesboro schools, she was taught well, and wanted to spend her life teaching others well.

All of her life, she wanted to be a teacher at Westside Middle School: that was her dream job, and she was living her dream.

It would be facile to say that saving a child's life is exactly what every teacher is supposed to do—and nobody wants America's teachers to go anywhere near such lengths in the pursuit of their professions. Most of the debate you hear now focuses on the violence, not the teaching. How to keep violence out of the classroom, how to keep schools safe. That is unquestionably the first, most pressing issue in this case.

And yet the symbolism keeps coming back to this reporter. Shannon Wright saved a student's life. Literally. Shannon Wright was a teacher. And to be a teacher is to give a young person the tools with which to build a life.

Your reporter feels strongly about such things, not only because I studied at a teachers college, but also because I feel so strongly, know so well, the debt I owe to my own teachers.

They never took a bullet for me. They were never called on to do so. It would be exaggerating to say they *saved* my life. And yet, they helped me to make something of my life.

My English teachers taught me to read and write—and kept after me to read more and write better. My journalism teachers taught me the rules of the craft I pursue to this day. My geography teachers taught me the names of all the places I'd one day visit. My science teachers taught me to experiment, my health teachers taught me to take care of myself.

Without my teachers, *all* of them, my life would be less— yes, and by now perhaps even lost.

Isn't the same true for you, too? It's true for most teachers.

Most American teachers are trying to help children make something of their lives. Most American teachers are trying with all their might, every day, whether or not anybody notices.

Can you wonder why that's what Shannon Wright wanted to do with *her* life? She was a hero—before she took that bullet.

Let's remember that—and learn from it.

Since this piece was written, the sort of tragedy it describes has become a disturbingly familiar story line: tragedies in Springfield, Oregon; Pearl, Mississippi; Littleton, Colorado; Los Angeles, California; and Fort Worth, Texas, have all seen children and the adults who teach and take care of them hurt and killed by guns.

IS THERE A CONDUCTOR IN THE HOUSE?
March 18, 1998

As recently as a century ago, if you wanted to hear music, you had better play or sing for yourself. If you wanted to hear more than that, you'd better have friends. If you wanted to hear an opera or symphony anytime you wanted to, you'd better be a king.

Today, of course, all we need to do is plug in the radio or stereo. One hundred, two hundred musicians at our command, any time of the day or night. In the car, at the gym, in the supermarket, anywhere we go, even places we don't want music. We can listen to musicians who aren't even alive anymore, from Patsy Cline to Elvis Presley to Maria Callas.

This reporter has gotten to wondering if our easy access to music has made it too easy for us to take music for granted.

Example: school districts feeling the pinch tend to cut music classes first, according to many experts. The reasoning apparently goes like this: music seems like a frivolity when you compare it to chemistry labs; instruments cost a lot of money (either to the school or to the parents); and, after all, why do you think they call it an "elective"?

Well, this happens to be a subject I know something about. You see, your reporter took music classes in public schools—the Houston Independent School District in Texas. Even then, I was no musical prodigy. They put me in the rhythm band and gave me a wood block to play. I wore it on a cord around my neck and hit it with a little stick.

Other children might have been expected to hit each other with the little stick. Not me. (Well, not often.) I was extremely respectful of my instrument. After all, the wood block is one of the world's oldest musical instruments. Scholars believe the wood block was invented *before* music. And if you needed proof of that, you had only to listen to the way I played.

About the best you could say for my performance was this: I very seldom played off-key.

I was also—don't ask how or why—assistant conductor of the William G. Love Elementary School band. To this day I can still conduct about three songs, just in case I'm at the concert hall one night and there's an emergency and somebody shouts: "Is there a conductor in the house?"

In all honesty, those little music classes didn't turn me into a musician—you'd need a *magician* to do that. But those classes *did* give me an appreciation of music.

One: music is difficult. It requires work and thought and sweat and inspiration. I haven't taken it for granted since.

Two: music is exciting. It is truly thrilling to be sitting in a group of musicians when you are all playing (more or less) the same piece of music: you are part of a great, powerful, vibrant entity. And nothing beats the feeling you get when you've practiced a difficult section over and over, and finally get it right. (Yes, even on the wood block.)

And if you think *you're* excited when you get that song right, imagine how your *mother* feels. You can see it in her face: relief and pride. Big pride.

Three: music is important. It says things your heart can't say any other way, and in a language everyone speaks. Music crosses borders, turns smiles to frowns, and vice-versa.

These observations are shared with a hope that, when schools cut back on music classes, they really think about what they're doing—and don't take music for granted.

RESPECT IN SCHOOLS
June 30, 1999

NEW YORK, NEW YORK—While we're thinking about what's wrong with our schools, consider this: the basics aren't the three "R's"—reading, 'riting, and 'rithmetic. There are *four*. The fourth "R" is respect.

These are the bedrocks of good schooling. Any school that emphasizes all four "R's"—really concentrates its efforts on having students excel in these areas—will shine. One of our most important national problems is that there are not enough community leaders, school principals, and teachers willing to dedicate themselves to an all-out, back-to-basics approach.

This isn't just the opinion of a wandering reporter. I've interviewed a number of very experienced principals and teachers in every major region of the country in recent months. And every one of them says a version of the same thing.

"At every level, in every grade, dedication—absolute dedication—and rock-hard resolve to emphasize the *four* 'R's' is the key to making schools better. And the fourth 'R'—respect—is every bit as important as the first three."

Example: a teacher in California says, "Everyone from the school board right on down through the ranks knows what's needed. But there's too much inertia and too much fear to make it a day-by-day policy, and to stick to it."

Fear?

"Yes," she says. "Everybody's afraid that parents won't support it, especially when it comes to respect. Parents often give lip service to it. But then when we try to teach and demand respect, they don't back us."

A principal in Texas says, "School superintendents and school boards regularly cave in to pressure from parents and threat of lawsuits. You try to really enforce discipline and hammer down on disrespect in a public school, you're asking for trouble. And you're going to get it."

One of the oldest and best teachers in New York agrees.

"Everybody talks about wanting to get back to basics, including teaching respect, but few are actually willing to pour themselves into making it happen. From elementary school teachers right on up through the system, and most especially including parents, the resolve to do it just isn't there."

In Louisiana, Governor Mike Foster and the state legislature are trying. They're putting in a new law that requires students to address teachers and other school employees respectfully.

Students must say "please," "thank you," "yes, ma'am," and "yes, sir"—whatever is appropriate. Those who don't follow this new mandated politeness can be punished. Just how severely will be left to local school districts to decide.

The idea has sparked a lot of jokes, and there are, of course, some critics who believe government has no right to enforce mores and attitudes by legislating what people say. Then there's the matter of the U.S. Constitution's First Amendment and its guarantee of freedom of speech.

But Governor Foster insists the law will help instill in children a habit of being respectful, something important that can carry over into later life.

He says, "If it's done in the right spirit, it will do a lot to help youngsters understand something that a lot of them are not taught at home."

He and others who support the effort are moving not a moment too soon. Louisiana public schools, along with those in New York City, are regularly judged to be among the worst in the nation.

Lack of respect among students certainly isn't the only problem. Lack of respect among parents is another. There is a need for new supplies—such as computers—and even buildings in many districts. Also, better pay and other incentives to get and keep better teachers is a widespread need.

But back to the core point: reform and improvement of the national treasure that is our public school system begins with a rededication to fundamentals. With special emphasis on the fourth "R."

BLACK HISTORY MONTH: AN AMERICAN EXPERIENCE, NOT A MARKETING CAMPAIGN
February 18, 1998

"Black History Month" is winding down. For some Americans, it's nothing more than a marketing campaign. But for millions of others, "Black History Month" is a time to reflect on the heart and soul of this nation's identity.

Your reporter was reminded of this while talking to an old friend, Clifford Alexander. A modern civil rights campaigner, he is himself a not-insignificant figure in black history.

He's sixty-four now. Tall, still handsome, with an easy smile and a commanding presence. It seems only yesterday that he was fresh out of Harvard, an aide in the Lyndon Johnson White House—one of the first blacks ever to hold such a high position in any administration. Under President Carter, Alexander served as the first black secretary of the army—and played a key role in promoting Colin Powell from colonel to general.

Black history is American history, Alexander says, because throughout our history this country has struggled with racial questions that began in the relationship between blacks and whites. The first question was whether "freedom for all" would apply to blacks in America. The answer was yes, but only after painful dispute. Now the question is how best to guarantee that freedom—and what it means.

"African Americans still can't hail a cab, or get and progress in a job, or buy a house or rent an apartment where they choose—not with the same ease as white Americans. This is disgraceful," Alexander says, slamming down his hand. "It is un-American. We all know it. But few want to face it, much less talk about it."

The conventional wisdom is that recent black history has been characterized by African Americans who succeed—but then fail to do anything to help other African Americans improve their economic lot.

Cliff Alexander stands in direct contrast to the stereotype. Today he runs his own company in Washington, is a sought-after policy analyst, is active in many charities, and sits on numerous corporate boards. There (and elsewhere) he tries to help people of all races get a fair shake.

Alexander grew up in Harlem. Although his family was prominent and well connected there, he knew plenty of prejudice as a young man.

"I've tried hard not to forget it, on the one hand, and on the other not to dwell on it. But mostly I have tried not to forget that many people still suffer from prejudice, and that most of them have much harder lives than mine."

He favors affirmative action, he says. "You bet I do. But not as any preference policy. Affirmative action plans are tools to create a fairer, more inclusive workplace and school. They aren't the only tools, but they are valuable ones. Affirmative action . . . is about fairness, equal opportunity, and how to achieve these goals."

The lifelong Democrat is critical of President Clinton. For

example, Alexander believes that, with pressure from the President, white boardrooms might create more equitable hiring and working conditions, and that the results would be seen from condominiums to classrooms throughout America.

"The President prays for change and talks about change, and I compliment him—up to a point—for that. But he isn't fully committed to making himself an agent for change, a great champion for racial fairness. That could be and should be Bill Clinton's historic mission as President. But he isn't going to do it. He either doesn't have the commitment or the courage—or both."

The President is only one American not living up to his potential; Cliff Alexander isn't letting many of us off the hook. But, he says, black history—and American history—are hanging in the balance.

WACO REVISITED
November 10, 1999

Like it or not, we're all soon going to be hearing a lot about various new investigations into the deaths at the Branch Davidian compound near Waco, Texas. All basically focus on two main questions:

Did the FBI or other government agencies fire into the compound during the last day of the standoff, just before or during the ultimate inferno?

And were U.S. military assets actively involved in the tactical operation that day? If so, were some of them from secret "special operations" military units? And, if so, who approved their participation?

The Davidian story climaxed six and a half years ago, in 1993, with the deaths of eighty people, many of them children.

The self-described religious group perished under the leadership of David Koresh, who died with his followers defying the law.

Previous investigations and the consensus of public opinion have concluded that Koresh was primarily responsible for his own and the other deaths in what amounted to a suicide pact.

But questions about what role the federal government could have—should have—played in averting the tragedy have lingered and grown.

One reason they have done so is evidence that has accumulated that various people in the government, especially in the FBI, might not have told the truth, the whole truth, and nothing but the truth.

Mark well the word "might." The FBI and others closely involved on the government side insist that they have told the truth and that they did their best to act in the public interest and carry out the law in a tough, dangerous situation.

It is their contention that radical-right "militia" and other groups, some of them racist and nearly all of them antigovernment are spreading rumors and fomenting doubt for their own highly partisan political and ideological purposes.

The FBI swears that none of its agents fired into the compound, and that it knows of no other government or law-enforcement agents who did. The U.S. military says the same thing.

The Defense Department did have "a few" military people on the scene—it says at the request of the FBI—to aid and support the Bureau with advice and equipment. But, the Pentagon insists, no military personnel were directly involved in attacking the compound.

The importance of the Pentagon's position is that U.S. law forbids direct military involvement in this kind of domestic law-enforcement operation—without the direct approval of the President or, at the very least, the secretary of defense.

So, it is argued by investigators, if the military was actively, directly involved in the assault on the Davidians, it either acted illegally or legal approval has been kept secret through lying. And that is a serious thing in a constitutional republic such as ours based on the rule of law—regardless of what Koresh and his Davidians did or did not do.

Any lying or other cover-up of such illegal acts would be a felony, and a very serious one in a country rooted in elected representative government. We require a high degree of trust and accountability from our leadership.

This is why we'll be hearing much from four separate investigations in the future: the special independent inquiry led by former Senator John Danforth; a subcommittee of the Senate Judiciary Committee headed by Pennsylvania Senator Arlen Specter (a former distinguished prosecutor); the House's Government Reform Committee chaired by Indiana Congressman Dan Burton; and lawyers from the Davidians, who have filed a wrongful-death suit against the government.

Politics, power, money, and ego are all heavily involved. So are some important questions.

A SYMBOL FILLS THE NEED OF
A NEW GENERATION
December 13, 1992

There's something about Malcolm X that makes reporters, especially white reporters, weigh their words. Even now. I expect he'd want it that way. We sit down at our word processors, and the ghost of Malcolm pops out: "Watch what you say. The people I care about don't need you, or your interpretations of what I've said or done."

I heard Malcolm speak—once. I was covering Martin Luther King, Jr., and the civil rights movement in the South. On a quick trip to New York I went along with a local WCBS-TV crew to cover one of Malcolm's speeches in Harlem.

His sentence structure was tight, his words direct, his message as blunt as a punch in the nose. Malcolm was angry, and he didn't leave you wondering why or whether his anger was justified, even when he was saying something that might not agree with what you'd always believed. Malcolm gave me a lot to squirm over and get hot about. He meant to make whites uncomfortable and blacks determined.

Back in Georgia, Dr. King asked me what I thought of this new preacher who was neither Southern nor Christian, whose thundering voice demanded attention and—increasingly—got it. I couldn't really make much answer, because I was still trying to comprehend what I'd heard. In many ways, I still am.

There's so much myth and mystery and so many messages to sift through—and there's so much reality that's beyond the comprehension and experience even of a reporter who likes to think he's reasonably seasoned—that I'm humbled.

I wouldn't presume to explain or interpret Malcolm X to anybody. But I have studied the facts, conducted extensive research and interviews. All I presume to do is to set forth what I've found.

What I've found is the symbolic appeal of Malcolm X. The man, the message, the myth are all important, but less important than what they have come to symbolize for some in a new generation of African Americans.

In his own way, Malcolm X became a political symbol—partly because of accident and circumstance, partly because of hard work. Malcolm X was and is a highly visible symbol for a few important ideas:

- *Self-reliance*. Malcolm was a survivor, with all the strength and confidence that come from getting through tough times. And when Malcolm needed to rely on others, he relied on blacks—his brothers and sisters, his wife, his mosque, his followers, his community.

- *Commitment to a lifetime of learning and personal growth.* In prison, following his conversion to Islam, Malcolm acquired something pretty close to a doctorate in philosophy, self-taught. The breadth and depth of his reading, his never-ending exploration of language, his mastery of the arts of rhetoric and debate would be invaluable tools in his later preaching and activism. It is Malcolm's command of language that affords him so much power twenty-seven years after his death. Some of the most stirring passages of his autobiography describe his transformation in prison from a kind of pacing, powerless animal to a ready angel of intellectual might.

- *The value of a "Don't Tread on Me—I Will Not Be Bullied" determination.* Malcolm X displayed it not only toward whites. He also showed this determination to the late Elijah Muhammad and to those disciples of the Chicagoan who tried to intimidate Malcolm. This kind of determination can, of course, be dangerous. In Malcolm's case, it led to his death. Whether we admire his philosophy or not, we admire his strength, his refusal to back down on matters that were important to him.

Yes, Malcolm did bad things, especially when he was young. He paid the penalty, renounced his wicked ways, and changed. His life became proof that white men lied when they said black men would not change. Lest we forget, that's what some whites were saying in the early sixties, to justify their failure to improve the condition of African-American life.

Yes, Malcolm said things that were hurtful, potentially destructive, and sometimes just plain wrongheaded.

And yes, there are some who are revising history and making the man into something he never was.

But recognizing all of that risks blinding us to the symbol Malcolm X has become.

He was a complicated man. He rose to stand for something and to urge others to stand for things—such as candor and courage, pride, and self-reliance.

Of such men and women, legends and then myths are sometimes made. There never has been a legend or myth without a flawed hero at its center. And there has never been a symbol without a need.

The preceding essay originally appeared in the Los Angeles Times.

THE HARD TRUTH ABOUT HARD DRUGS
August 20, 1997

Cops, both on the line and undercover, those down where the work is gritty and dangerous, will tell you things the politicians won't. Such as: we are *not* winning the fight against big-time drug dealing.

You may have read recent headline stories about Mexican drug lords pouring cocaine and marijuana into the U.S. The trouble with those stories, cops and others tell me, is that they are such a small part of the dismal overall picture that they can distort and mislead.

Classic middlemen, Mexican operators basically *transport* cocaine and heroin for Colombian syndicates. Some have developed their own selling webs, mostly in the West. And now, according to the spate of recent stories, experienced drivers of big tractor-trailer trucks in Michigan have been recruited by Mexican syndicates to haul narcotics from Mexico to eastern metropolitan areas.

Overall and in the main, Colombians still overwhelmingly control production and the U.S. sales networks. What's new about Mexican syndicates is that they are transporting more for the Colombians than they once did, and they are doing it all over America.

What else is new, and ominous, is that Colombians have branched out, rapidly rising as suppliers and marketers of heroin.

Cocaine and marijuana remain a major problem in America, but skyrocketing use of heroin, especially among the young, is the big news now.

This is not the heroin of the sixties and seventies. It is far stronger, addicting more, faster. And because Colombia is pouring in so much of it, it is far cheaper on the street than ever. A much more potent product at drastically reduced prices equals a boom in sales. Especially among America's youth.

Besides the boom in heroin, the widening Mexican drug transportation systems, and increased Colombian supply, another underreported reality of the drug trade in America is the rise of gangs in dealing heroin.

The subculture of gangs has grown tremendously in recent years, and not just in their traditional strongholds of San Francisco, Los Angeles, New York, and Philadelphia.

With their growth has come greater involvement in the distribution and marketing of heroin. For example, drug enforcement pros on the streets say Chinese gangs are recruiting former convicts from America's many prisons. Black Muslims with long prison records appear to be favored as regional and local drug captains by the biggest Chinese gangs.

There was a time when the word on the street was that Chinese gangs were especially distrustful and suspicious of African-American gangs, and vice-versa. They did little business with each other.

The same was true of Hispanic gangs. But as Hispanic and Chinese gangs got more involved in drug trafficking, the number of their members caught and sent to prison increased. Inside prisons, Chinese and Hispanic gang members came to believe that African Americans who are Muslims would make prime partners in crime. True, Islam has numerous prohibitions against drug use or trade. But then, so does Christianity.

Beware of stereotyping when considering all of this. Many, if not most, of the biggest drug profiteers—seldom publicly identified or caught—are white. White Americans in large measure finance the despicable narcotics trade. Whites put up the capital; they launder the profits. That's true around the world, and in our own country.

It is also true that 70 percent of drug *users* in this country are white.

America is, by far, the largest market in the world for illegal narcotics. We have the most users and abusers. We have the biggest profiteers. And, say the men and women on the front lines of the losing war against drugs, most of those in this made-in-the-U.S.A. problem are *not* people of color.

The drug situation in Colombia has gotten darker in even the short time since this column was written. Revolutionaries in the north of the country have forged an alliance with local drug lords, offering them protection from the government in return for big-time funding for their guerrilla war. All this has brought fears of a narcostate emerging in Central America, and calls for a major push to aid the present Colombian regime.

PHOENIX LOOKS FOR SOLUTIONS
April 15, 1998

PHOENIX, ARIZONA—When an out-of-towner comes to this sun-splashed city, violence seems as remote as a rainy day. But for Arizonans, as for most Americans, violence is a more frequent reality than surface impressions suggest. This is especially true for children.

Children commit a shocking number of violent crimes today, and have a shocking number of crimes committed against them.

It's true in Phoenix and most places large and small all over the country.

This reporter came here to take part in a town meeting on children and violence, sponsored in part by *The Arizona Republic*. The session unfolded in the Orpheum, a beautifully restored old theater, packed with citizens from every walk of life.

There was the usual blaming of the media, sports, and parents—for setting bad examples, for not doing enough to be role models, and for glamorizing violence.

But, as one member of the audience said, "Let's stop placing blame and start talking about what can be done."

Dawon Coleman spoke up. He's a former member of the Insane Crips gang, and now works with a Youth Outreach program. Coleman thinks most Americans have no idea how influential gangs have become.

"Parents, schools, and communities at large must intervene in the lives of gang members and other at-risk kids," he says. "They need to make sure there are a lot of alternatives to gang activity—and they need to guide kids into those alternatives. That's absolutely essential."

One of pro football's top receivers, Rob Moore of the Arizona Cardinals, said he thinks "lack of emphasis on discipline" and "lack of the kind of structure team sports can give to their lives" lead many kids into overly aggressive behavior.

Parents and educators—and young people, including one outspoken seventeen-year-old volunteer from a local high school—urged adults to get children out from in front of the television set. And they agreed it's not enough merely to turn off the set. Kids need to be doing something positive with their time.

Several people urged youngsters to get into the habit of attending church or other religious services.

We talked about lengthening the school day and the school year. The thinking is that if parents work, and kids are getting out of school at two or three in the afternoon, there are several hours without supervision, when kids could be getting into trouble—drugs, crime, sex, and yes, violence.

Wouldn't lengthening the school day and the school year limit the amount of unsupervised time children spend, and thus limit the risk? And at the same time, couldn't children continue learning?

The town meeting was attended by several educators and experts, but some were hesitant to endorse this idea.

"How many children are in the audience?" asked Dr. Kay Rauth-Farley with a laugh. She added that she didn't think that more class time was necessarily the answer, but that other kinds of activities, sports and recreation, might help—and do help in many communities.

Jane Dee Hull, governor of Arizona, listened to it all. She patiently took criticism, including some that state agencies were sometimes too slow, too insensitive, and too uncoordinated to help abused kids and those in other kinds of trouble.

A mother and grandmother, the governor vowed that Arizona will do better—pronto. She has already made reducing youth violence a top priority.

"You come back in a year," she told me, "and we're going to be better, a lot better. We're getting more of every community involved every day."

And so it went deep into the night. Is it just a desert mirage, this seemingly increased awareness about kids and violence in America?

One wonders, and worries.

LESSONS OF AN AMERICAN SON
January 27, 1997

A friend gave me a call yesterday. Could I come over? The Super Bowl was coming on, he said, and he was feeling lonely. The Super Bowl, you see, was something he and his son used to watch together. And now his son is dead. The shock of his son's death hasn't even worn off—but now the shock of his son's absence causes deeper pain. There was an empty space on the sofa, one that can't ever be filled again.

My friend's son was shot and killed several days ago. There are a few clues, and the police are determined to find the killer. They're hearing from all kinds of people—fellow citizens, neighbors—who may know something, who want to help. My friend says he believes the killer or killers will be found. He says he wants justice. His wife just wants to get the killer, just *get* them.

He and his wife are trying to heal, trying to learn from their loss. The ancient Greeks taught us that there are lessons in life that can best be understood in death. And my friend's son was profoundly interested in lessons.

He was a teacher. He was studying to become a better teacher. This was already an accomplishment, because my friend's son had learning disabilities that could easily have derailed his education. But my friend's son had teachers who understood the problem, and parents who loved him. And, perhaps most important, my friend's son found within himself the resources he needed. He studied. He learned. And he wanted to help other children, like the child he once was. Children for whom learning was a real challenge. He knew that education is no less important, when it's more difficult.

Since my friend's son died, I've read some of the things he wrote about growing up with learning disabilities. About learning. About teaching. He was already a great teacher, in a field where this country desperately needs good teachers.

Special education programs can be expensive; they can also be among the first to be cut back in school districts facing tough budgets. If the death of my friend's son serves one purpose—to remind us of the value and importance of special education—then his spirit may rest more easily.

Ennis Cosby will be missed. His parents, Bill and Camille, already miss him. So should we. Not because his father is a famous man, but because Ennis Cosby had a handle on what's important in life. He made a difference. He was ready to make a bigger difference.

JON-BENET'S PICTURES
January 8, 1997

By now we are all familiar with the murder case of little Jon-Benet Ramsey of Boulder, Colorado. Too familiar. And that's the problem.

There is so little to tell about this story. A little girl is dead who shouldn't be, and we don't know yet who killed her. The night of her death, she was sexually abused, presumably by her killer. And that's the whole story. However, just about every news organization, including this one, has been reporting the story at greater length than the facts so far really warrant, as if nothing else of importance were happening in the world.

We are all trying to derive some meaning from the life and death of this little girl. But we are trying in a strange way.

There may or may not be any connection between her abuse and murder, and the fact that little Jon-Benet was a beauty pageant prodigy. Because there's no case, because there are no suspects, we can't be certain that Jon-Benet's hobby had anything to do with her death.

So why do news organizations keep showing the pictures?

Admit it: you know exactly which pictures I'm talking about. Little Jon-Benet wearing very grown-up makeup. Sequined outfits like a showgirl. Dance moves that are, to use a nice word, sophisticated. Song lyrics about how much she wants a boyfriend.

Maybe Jon-Benet would've been better advised to sing "On the Good Ship Lollipop" in tap shoes, but there's no question the little girl was a born performer and, for all we know, enjoyed performing, enjoyed competing in pageants.

What we don't know, what we can't know, is whether any of that had anything to do with her abuse and murder. The simple ugly fact is that, every year, children who don't wear sequins and makeup are abused and killed.

So why are we looking at Jon-Benet's pictures?

The wise owls and pundits show us the pictures and cluck over them: "See what a sign of our sick society this is," they say. "How can you expect any happy outcome, when you doll up little girls like sex objects?"

They may have a point. But all the while they're trying to make that point, they're showing the pictures. And we're looking. Not as if we were peeping at a carnival sideshow, but as if we were doing something ennobling, helping society by staring at the pictures.

Just by looking at those pictures, just by dwelling so long on this sad, sad story—before we even know very much about it—we're saying more about our society than the wise owls and pundits ever do.

The Jon-Benet Ramsey story lives on in the media. The most recent bit of non-news came on November 13, 1999, when the grand jury in the case announced that it would not hand down an indictment. After some consideration, the town of Boulder, Colorado, decided against hiring a special investigator to look into the case further. Cost of the investigation so far: $2 million.

ROBBER BARONS OF THE INFORMATION AGE?
December 3, 1997

Bill Gates and Microsoft are a great American success story. Detractors, not all of them just envious, are beginning to build a case for a dark side to the story.

The heart of their claim is: Bill Gates is a 1990s version of "the Robber Barons."

The term originated with those few, very wealthy Americans who, at the turn of the twentieth century, had a stranglehold on key businesses of the Industrial Age.

Their hold was so complete that it was nearly impossible for anyone to compete with them. When it came to steel, oil, banking, and other cores of the newly booming Industrial Age, the Rockerfellers, the Carnegies, and a few others had a hammerlock.

They were, in many ways, stronger, more powerful than the U.S. government. They were a kind of nation unto themselves, answerable to no one.

It wasn't until the early 1900s, when the Progressive Republican reform movement and Presidents Theodore Roosevelt and William Howard Taft led a backlash, that the Robber Barons were even challenged.

After a fierce fight, new antitrust laws were finally passed to bust up the cartels. These laws opened competition. That led to fresh flows of entrepreneurial capital. And all of this helped build an American economy that made the U.S. a world leader through out the century.

Now, as we begin the turn into the twenty-first century, has another, similar stranglehold developed in America on key businesses of the Information Age?

It's possible. James Gleick of the *New York Times* and some other writers on the subject are convinced. They cast Microsoft, Gates, and his close allies as the new Robber Barons, ruthless rajahs of the computer kingdom. Or at least having the potential, the will, and the ways to become such.

That's what this month's federal court hearing concerning Microsoft is about. Specifically, the claim that Gates and Microsoft have snookered the U.S. government and the people of the United States—again. And that they have done so illegally—again.

After dallying for what critics see as far too long, the Justice Department's Antitrust Division finally moved against some of Gates's computer software monopoly maneuvers in 1994. Specifically, they objected to the way Microsoft tied the integration of Windows 95 exclusively to the later, secondary Internet Explorer system.

Again, as critics view it, the Justice Department was not only late, it was dumb. The people's antitrust lawyers struck an agreement with Microsoft that was virtually "toothless," in Gleick's view. So "toothless," Gleick says, that Bill Gates publicly boasted the agreement meant "nothing" and wouldn't affect the company's business practices.

However weak and meek the agreement may have been, Gates and Microsoft didn't live up to it. They went on merrily with their choke-hold ways against all competition to their worldwide computer software products.

Or so the Justice Department and Gates's competitors claim. Which is why they are back in court this month.

Fairness dictates that it be pointed out that Gates, Microsoft, and some experts in the field strongly deny the charges against the company.

Their story is: Gates and Microsoft are simply better and smarter than everybody else in the business. And they are just reaping the benefits, fair and square.

We are not likely to have conclusive answers to all of this until sometime early in the next century.

So far, Gates and Microsoft have the whip hand. No big public backlash has developed. No new Progressive Republican (or Democratic) movement has emerged. Nor has any crusading President. And there are no new "break up the cartels" antitrust laws in the making for the dawn of the Information Age.

> *At the time of this revision, the writing is on the wall for the verdict in the Microsoft antitrust case. In a November 5, 1999, ruling on "findings of fact," Judge Thomas Penfield Jackson set the stage by stating that the government had proved that Microsoft was a competition-thwarting monopoly. As observers have pointed out, however, this is a case that will no doubt be ultimately decided on appeal . . . the conclusion of which could come years from this writing.*

SONGBIRD OF THE SMOKIES
May 6, 1998

BLACKBERRY HILL, TENNESSEE—I grew up listening to something called "hillbilly music." In my lifetime, those sounds metamorphosed to "cowboy music" and then to "country" or "country and western." What's never changed is the honesty.

Other kinds of music don't have to be honest, or even realistic. Americans who listen to country music also live it, and they demand the same of the musicians.

Real-life American love stories aren't fairy tales, and you won't find many princes of the blood royal driving eighteen-wheelers cross-country at three o'clock in the morning (the optimum way to listen to country music).

The best country musicians are like good reporters: they tell it like it is. The late Tammy Wynette was one of the breed. Her ex-husband, George Jones, is another. So are Johnny Cash and Loretta Lynn, as were Hank Williams and Patsy Cline before them.

And then there's Dolly Parton. Her voice is so sweet, sometimes you forget she's telling you the truth. She's so glamorous, sometimes you forget she's a sharecropper's daughter, granddaughter of a Pentecostal preacher, from Pigeon Forge, Tennessee.

Dolly hasn't forgotten. "I've never left the Smoky Mountains," she says. "I've taken them with me wherever I go."

She believes she grew up at one with the earth, watched over by God. "We had a great love for nature," she recalls, "which meant we had a great love for God." That's why, although she could live anywhere in the world, she comes back to the hills and hollers where she grew up, and where she met me this misty spring morning.

"How can you just walk around and see these birds and see this grass, these hills—and if you believe in anything, you have to see God right here. I just see Him, I feel Him, I just feel I can touch Him, and I know He touches me through all this."

From childhood, everything seemed to make music for Dolly. She tells me that the first time she heard Hank Williams's classic "I'm So Lonesome I Could Cry," she could hear the call of whippoorwills in the song. Naturally, she wound up singing along.

"My grandpa believed that you could make a joyful noise unto the Lord, and whatever you was banging on was all right with God," she recalls. She demonstrates by playing her hit "9 to 5," anthem of the working woman, on her fingernails. "It sounded like a typewriter, so it inspired me." She grins. "When you love music, you can make it out of anything."

She's heard the tired complaint that country songs are too sad. "What do you get when you play a country song backwards?" she says, quoting the old joke: "You get your wife back, and you get your dog back, that whole thing." She rolls her eyes.

She sings from the heart because she doesn't know any other way. If she's sad, she isn't going to deny it as a part of life, any more than she's going to deny beauty or love. It's natural.

"The way I grew up, I remember all the sadness, not just my own but my parents' sadness when people would die, or when crops would fail, when things were really hard and somebody was sick," she says. "I took all that to heart, and I made a living out of it, too, by putting it into songs."

Looking out over Dolly Parton's "Tennessee Home" (to borrow from the title of another of her hit songs), it's easy to understand why for her, music and nature and God are all one thing—and a song runs through it.

THE AIR-CONDITIONED AMERICAN DREAM
July 2, 1998

You talk about your long, hot summers. Mark this one for your grandchildren. You pick up the paper, turn to the weather map, and all you see is red. (Even in black-and-white papers!)

Nowhere has the map been redder than Texas. More than half a month straight of triple-digit temperatures in Dallas. And Dallas is in *north* Texas.

General William Tecumseh Sherman knew this. Which is why, after his short service in the Lone Star State, he said: "If I owned Hell and Texas, I'd live in Hell and rent out Texas."

So how do people there stand it? Two words: air conditioning. Without modern air conditioning, Texas would still be mostly just cow and cactus country.

Instead, Texas is now more urban than rural, the third most populous state in the union, with four of the nation's largest and fastest-growing big cities (Houston, Dallas, San Antonio, and El Paso).

Air conditioning made it so. Just as it has created the boom in the Sun Belt, the entire southern half of the country, since World War II.

Miami, Atlanta, Charlotte, Albuquerque, Phoenix, Palm Springs, southern California—without air conditioning, none of them become what they are today.

Keep in mind that it isn't just the American population shift to the Sun Belt that has hallmarked the last fifty years. With the population movement has come a shift in the nation's whole political center of gravity.

Without air conditioning, it is unlikely that Lyndon Johnson, Richard Nixon, Jimmy Carter, Ronald Reagan, George Bush, or Bill Clinton would have been President. No Speaker Gingrich, either. These politicians didn't spring from the sweltering backwoods.

Before air conditioning, if you ran into a heat wave such as the one that's borne down on the Sun Belt this summer, you had few options: you moved away, you curtailed all activity, or you *died*. You did not have the option of building up a significant power base.

There's an argument to be made that air conditioning should take its place beside the atomic bomb, the pill, penicillin, transistors, and microchips as one of the most important American developments of the midcentury.

Humans have been trying to cool the air since ancient times, using primitive evaporation devices (wet mats suspended in doorways) and fans (palm leaves). Leonardo da Vinci (who else?) built the first mechanical fan around 1500. Americans began experimenting with air conditioning in the nineteenth century, as New Englanders made extensive efforts to humidify the air in their textile mills.

Who actually developed modern air conditioning as we

know it? It depends which manufacturer you ask: everybody seems to want credit. Most outside observers (call them "cooler heads") give the nod to Willis H. Carrier. Carrier's science and engineering in the early 1900s led designers to the first electrical air conditioning worthy of the name.

Warm-weather air conditioning began to catch on with the wealthy about 1920, when reliable refrigeration machinery began to be manufactured in the post–World War I boom.

American ingenuity in automatic refrigeration compressors, controls, and thermal insulation quickly followed. But the Great Depression of the 1930s slowed demand and manufacture. That gave Americans time to refine their technology.

And when World War II was over, air conditioning manufacturers could capitalize not only on big, newly prosperous markets at home and abroad, but also on a manufacturing infrastructure left over from the war years.

First homes and workplaces, then cars became air-conditioned in the 1950s and 60s. That's when the Sun Belt population and political shift took off.

And that's when the American Dream went to MAX A/C.

OKLAHOMA EXPLOSION
April 19, 1995

A disaster as sudden as the terrorist bombing of the Alfred P. Murrah Federal Building in Oklahoma City isn't conducive to measured response, careful thought, or crafted language. I am grateful to my colleague Greg Kandra for writing this report, which would be for many radio listeners the first news of the tragedy. Among Greg's gifts is the ability to allow the ear to see the story:

his descriptions remain among the most powerful and sensitive I have ever read.

April, the poet wrote, is the cruelest month. And this April morning, cruelty rained down on Oklahoma City.

The devastation was swift, sudden, stunning. Half a federal office building shattered: walls and floors and windows decimated, as if a huge hand had simply clawed them away. Men and women, and even children, were left stained with blood, dazed, walking the streets in shock and disbelief.

Others remained trapped in the rubble, crawling toward daylight, desperate for rescuers they could not reach. It will be hours, if not days, before the full extent of this tragedy is known.

Some observers compared what they saw to the bombing of the American embassy in Beirut, more than a decade ago. Others could not help but hear echoes of the World Trade Center bombing, two years ago.

But that was Beirut, and New York. This was Oklahoma.

For whatever unfathomable reason, terror has come home to the heartland.

Authorities took notice, and took action. Other federal buildings around the nation were cleared and closed. Anxiety climbed, nerve endings frayed: if it could happen in Oklahoma, the reasoning went, it could happen anywhere.

And with that, another chilling truth took hold: there are no more sanctuaries, no more safe havens, no place to hide.

All day, experts have struggled to answer the word on everyone's lips: why? Why now, why here? Why were so many of the victims small children, from a day care center?

Was it an attack from the Jihad . . . or a commemoration of the Waco tragedy, two years ago today . . . or a link to yet another unknown terrorist cell, buried in the darkest part of America's heart?

At this hour, they are questions without answers.

We live in an age without reason, when cults attack subway trains, when unholy acts are committed in the name of holy causes. The world has been twisted into a strange and unfamiliar shape by bombings and gunfire and poison.

And it has now reached Oklahoma on an April morning fresh with the promise of spring—a promise suddenly clouded by smoke, and sorrow, and fear.

VICTIMS AFTER THE VERDICT
June 2, 1997

Headline of the day: a Denver jury has found Timothy McVeigh guilty of all charges in the bombing of the federal building in Oklahoma City. Sentencing in the trial is scheduled to begin on Wednesday; the death penalty is a possibility.

Timothy McVeigh was identified as a suspect, but he was never thrown to the mob. He was allowed to defend himself in open hearing, to question his accusers. The United States government, the target of his attack, paid for Timothy McVeigh's defense attorneys, and indeed for the entire case, over $50 million and counting. His innocence was defended until a jury of his peers determined that he was guilty beyond a reasonable doubt. That's the American way.

This chapter in this sad, sad story is over. But McVeigh is expected to appeal the verdict. There will be more chapters; the story will go on—for McVeigh, for the jurors, and for the victims.

Susan Walton, for example. She doesn't think of herself as a victim, no sir. She is strong: her life continues, full steam ahead.

You see Susan Walton just outside the courthouse in Denver. You can't take your eyes off her. You want to weep. As a reporter, you've covered wars, famines, epidemics, and disasters for a lifetime. Your job is not to show emotion. Just get the facts.

But, face to face with this woman, it takes all you can muster to fight back tears.

Her body was shattered in the Oklahoma City bombing. Two years later, she is still in a wheelchair. She probably will be in one for the remainder of her days. Her legs are gone. So is one of her eyes. A darkened lens in her glasses covers that wound. Her whole face is disfigured. Her body will never again be what it was.

"I try not to dwell on it," she says. "I guess I'm angry, but I think that would be a negative in helping me to heal. So I try to look for positives."

You turn away, so that she won't see your tears. She doesn't need them: they're not positive.

To Timothy McVeigh, the target in Oklahoma City was "the government" and not people with families, stories, faces.

Susan Walton's face tells a different story. So does P. J. Allen's. P.J. was twenty months old, in the day care center when the Alfred P. Murrah Federal Building exploded. His tiny body was pierced repeatedly with fragments of metal and glass. He was burned over 90 percent of his body, then buried in an avalanche of concrete. When rescuers finally dug him out, they carried him to safety, limp and screaming. A miracle of God and good doctors has kept him alive. But just barely. Even now, two years later, P.J. remains in critical condition on a respirator. His life is always on the line. He could be dead by the time you read this.

I saw him shortly after the bombing. I still see him in my mind's eye, like a constantly replaying videotape. His grandmother, Mrs. Dolores Watson, told me this week, "I just keep praying."

For her, for P.J., for Susan Walton, the story of the bombing will never end. The verdict in the McVeigh trial is the end of one chapter, but not the end of the whole story.

Justice is like that. It's meant to bring closure, to answer questions, to put limits on our suffering, to stop the wrong-doing. The reality is often more complicated than that.

According to the ancient Greek playwright Aeschylus, jury trials were invented to replace vengeance with justice, to stop the cycle of killing so that life could go on.

For the victims of the Oklahoma City bombing and their families, these are not abstract issues. And because, in a real sense, the attack on the Federal Building was an attack on all of us, on all law-abiding Americans and our government, these are not abstract issues for you, for me, or for any American.

And so, the victims might have answered violence with violence. Instead, for the past two years they allowed the legal system to track down, to try, and then to punish the guilty. Now that the verdict has been handed down, life must go on.

For the victims, for all of us, life will go on with visible reminders of the losses: with scars of the flesh, and empty chairs at the table.

But there will be invisible reminders, too, of 168 lives cut short: scars we can't see, empty places we can't point to.

We will think of those men, women, and children of Oklahoma City. We will think of them often. We will recall the promise of those lives. And we will wonder—what might have been?

That's a question no jury can ever answer.

THE NEXT TRIAL
September 17, 1997

Now it's Terry Nichols's turn to face a jury for charges in the Oklahoma City bombing. Make no mistake: he will be harder to convict than Timothy McVeigh. A lot harder. Most lawyers and journalists believe this.

On his farm in Michigan, Terry's older brother, James, is saying so flatly.

Tim McVeigh lived with James Nichols for a while in Michigan. Which is why I went there to interview him. The FBI suspected James of being connected to the Oklahoma City bombing. They still do. But suspicion is one thing, proof quite another. The FBI arrested James but never charged him.

"They never charged me because I didn't do anything," James said during our daylong talks last year.

"And neither did my brother Terry. Sure, Terry knew McVeigh. So did I. But that doesn't mean we had anything to do with Oklahoma City. Terry wasn't there. Neither was I."

James was the first to use as a mantra the sentence "Terry wasn't there." Now Terry's defense team has adopted it. The jury will have it resounding in their ears when Terry's trial begins later this month (September 29, 1997).

"Terry wasn't there." It is the key difference between this case and McVeigh's.

Nichols has an alibi. McVeigh had none. Witnesses say that on the day of the bombing, Nichols was at his home in Herington, Kansas.

With McVeigh, there were direct links to the crime, such as his renting the bomb truck, and the residue from explosive materials found on his clothes. With Nichols, there are alleged links, but they are less direct, not as clear, and harder to prove.

The government will seek to prove Nichols helped plan the bombing, helped make the bomb, and helped position McVeigh's getaway car in Oklahoma City.

Twenty-seven acts leading to the bombing have been identified as "overt and decisive," and the government claims that in fifteen of those acts, Nichols acted either alone or with McVeigh.

Nichols's lead defense attorney, Michael Tigar, will try to

convince the jury that Nichols broke with McVeigh long before the bombing.

No one denies that Nichols and McVeigh knew a lot about
fertilizer bombs. They learned from James Nichols, on his
Michigan farm.

There's no easy way to reach the place. You fly to Saginaw,
then drive north for two hours. The farm is two hundred acres
of not the best land. James Nichols farms some of it, some of
the time. Much of the rest of his time he used to spend con-
testing the legitimacy of the United States government: filing
to renounce his citizenship, refusing to carry a driver's license,
and keeping tabs on the militia movement.

Neighbors report there have been many explosions on Nichols's farm. He says they exaggerate. But, he says, he has experimented with various forms of explosives. Why? "To get
the soybeans out of my grain bin, which is a normal practice
of farmers." (His neighbors say they don't set explosives to
loosen stored soybeans.)

Brother Terry and McVeigh both experimented with explosives when they were last at the farm, in 1994, James says.

But it was just small stuff, firecrackers and pop bottles, he
insists. "Kid's play, that's all it was. Purely, simply kid's play."

Then who *did* kill those 168 men, women, and children in
Oklahoma City?

"Show me one government that has never abused its citizens," says James Nichols. "Citizens to the government mean
nothing, are just property. And they can destroy them at will
or do whatever they wish, at will, with their property."

An interviewer presses: "Are you kidding? You really believe this?"

"I'm serious. I mean, why not? Truth is stranger than fiction."

*A jury of Terry Nichols's peers concluded that the
government was not the murderer in Oklahoma City,*

and that Terry Nichols bore responsibility for 168 deaths. He was convicted of conspiracy. A judge sentenced him to life in prison on June 4, 1998. An appeals court upheld the decision and the sentence on February 26, 1999.

JOHN GLENN
October 21, 1998

HOUSTON—John Glenn is a good, brave man who has given much to his country.

Whether he and NASA have made the right decision in sending Glenn back into space is an open question. It is, at least, among more people than are willing to publicly admit it.

The question hangs out there because Glenn's mission is part science and part publicity stunt.

Glenn is eager to talk about the science part of it, what such a trip can teach about aging and medicine. He is reluctant, sometimes even dismissive, when the talk gets around to the publicity aspects.

He shouldn't be. There is nothing wrong with seeking publicity for a good cause. The future of this country as a space-faring nation is, many of us believe, a good cause.

Glenn doesn't talk about it, but what may be somewhere in the back of his mind is the mistake NASA and the late astronaut Alan Shepard made. Shepard, you may recall, was America's first man in space. (Glenn, just after him, was the first American to orbit the Earth.) Shepard retired from the space program but later came back, begging for a chance to walk on the moon.

NASA gave him a moon shot. Trouble was, once on the

moon, Shepard pulled out a golf club and spent time demonstrating his favorite sport on the lunar surface. For what purpose, it was unclear.

What soon did become clear was that Shepard and NASA had blundered. The pictures of Shepard and his moon golf became campaign posters for those who opposed continuing to spend large sums for space exploration, especially further adventures to the moon.

"You see," went the arguments, "it is a waste of money, all of these manned trips up there. This guy piddling around with his golf shot is a perfect demonstration, a metaphor we can all understand. Whatever we do from now on in space—and we ought to do a lot less—should concentrate on *un*manned flights." So said the detractors and doubters.

Not long after Shepard's excursion in the early 1970s, trips to the moon ceased. NASA was already having funding problems. It got worse. There were many reasons for this, including President Richard Nixon's lack of interest in space exploration and a basic disbelief in its importance.

There was much talk of "On to Mars!" just after the first manned moon landing in 1969. By the mid-1970s, it was gone. And NASA descended into having to fight ever harder for money just to keep operating in any meaningful way.

So one can forgive John Glenn for being touchy when the publicity-seeking aspects of his mission are questioned.

Glenn is always at his best when talking about the future of exploring the cosmos and why Americans should continue to be big dreamers and big doers up on the high frontier.

When your reporter sat down with him recently at his Houston training headquarters, he jumped at the chance to talk about humans going to Mars. Yes, he believes such trips are inevitable. No, he is not sure it will happen in his lifetime.

"Let's see. Do I think humans will be on Mars in, say, the next twenty to twenty-five years? Well, I'm just not sure. I hope so. But there is still so much to be done, so many more steps in between. And it *will* take money."

So he leaves it at that. He knows how hard getting the money will be. Brave John Glenn has made of himself a pretty good politician since his former astronaut days. He has learned well the politician's code that "discretion is often the better part of valor." Especially when you're talking about the need for money.

But it's still true, Glenn is a better dreamer and doer than he is a talker. Which is why most of America will be pulling for him when he goes up for his victory lap in space, and murmuring once again, "Godspeed, John Glenn."

SEND DOOBIE
July 16, 1997

The space program never seemed more like a joke than it did in the summer of 1997. Unfortunately, the punch line had the potential to be seriously unfunny. While Americans and Russians struggled to hold together the aging Mir *space station, late-night comics laughed—lives were at stake—and the future of manned space exploration hung in the balance.*

I had a simple solution to the problem.

For weeks the world has watched a sorry spectacle. The *Mir* space station has been breaking down, lives are at stake, and Russian mission controllers have had to beg and plead to get anyone even to consider going up to make repairs. Evidently, any space mechanics in Russia or America are underqualified, or overscared, or too busy catching up on their suntans.

Frustrating. Potentially tragic. You want to tell 'em, "Send Doobie."

Doobie Rogers, that is: the pride of Pin Oak Creek, Texas,

and the best shade-tree mechanic anyplace west of A. J. Foyt's garage.

He's getting on in years now. Claims to be seventy-three, but suspicion is that he's run his age back a few years so he can keep himself employed. Doesn't look like much, old Doobie. Short, with a beer gut. Never did like to shave. When he's working hard, which is always, he sweats plenty. He chews tobacco whenever he isn't smoking. And he limps some, a result of an old workover oil rig that fell on his leg years ago.

So, no, he doesn't make an ideal first impression. But when it comes to fixing things, neither Maytag, nor Mack, nor Caterpillar ever made a machine Doobie couldn't fix.

He's a throwback to another time, a time when there were only two kinds of people in America: those who fixed and those who threw away. Doobie is a fixer. Had to be. He grew up in East Texas, where nobody had much but their pride. They learned to take care of what little they had.

Doobie grew up fascinated by machines. If it was a gadget with moving parts, Doobie studied it, took it apart, and put it back together. And in so doing, he learned how to repair it.

His pickup truck looks like a refugee from a demolition derby, but it hums like a sewing machine. I guarantee you he can take it apart, every piece, and put it back together again in one day.

On any workday, he arrives on the job with a metal toolbox that looks like something that should be in the Smithsonian. There's not a lot in it. Just the fundamentals: a ball-peen hammer, a hacksaw, screwdrivers, and a few wrenches. In a bag, he carries STP, WD-40, and his welding helmet.

But with these simple tools, Doobie works miracles.

Which is why I'm recommending him to our Russian space partners. When anything goes haywire with the *Mir,* they should just send Doobie. He may not speak Russian, but he'll get the job done. Pronto. And he'll clean up when he's done.

Let's face it. The *Mir* is not some sleek *Star Trek* spacecraft.

It's a contraption. Every time somebody goes up, they stick another section on it. Well, contraptions are Doobie's specialty.

I asked Doobie what the *Mir's* trouble was. "It's electrical," he said flatly. Stands to reason: if the lights don't work, the trouble must be electrical. Why bother consulting all those hesitating Soviet-era engineers?

Good mechanics, Mr. Fix-its, tinkerers with a beat-up toolbox and above-average curiosity, used to keep this country running. They invented the airplane and the lightbulb, refined the automobile, and propelled the United States to economic success. They also pointed the way to space.

Now we're deep into space, and competent mechanics of any kind are as rare as yellow-fronted bower birds. If it weren't for Doobie Rogers and a few like him, the tough jobs would be left undone—all over the galaxy.

So, take note, Mr. Yeltsin. The next time that rattling, clanking *Mir* goes on the blink—send Doobie.

SWEET LIBERTY
July 1, 1998

It's sad but true that many Americans celebrating this July Fourth don't know what's being celebrated.

This comes to mind as one ponders two of this week's headlines: President Clinton's trip to China, and the official word that the identity of the Unknown Soldier of the Vietnam War is no longer unknown.

The President used his China trip to speak forcefully about American values, specifically freedom. He did so after what many people considered an unnecessary kowtow to his dictator hosts at Tiananmen Square.

This appearance was a sacrilege of sorts, since the same Communist hierarchy had murderously mauled a movement for freedom and democracy centered in that very square in 1989.

But after giving his hosts the photo-op they wanted at Tiananmen Square—Mr. Clinton began speaking about the values most dear to Americans.

Presidents must speak of the great subjects of our Republic. Sadly, few do it often.

When Abraham Lincoln spoke at Gettysburg, he set the example. Lincoln reminded his audience (and every subsequent generation of Americans) of the purpose of the Civil War—and, indeed, of the purpose of the United States.

He sought to dedicate a military cemetery, although he conceded that "in a larger sense, we cannot dedicate—we cannot consecrate—we cannot hallow this ground." The soldiers who "gave their last full measure of devotion" had already done so, he said.

It was a speech for the ages, an eloquent statement of the American Spirit.

Lincoln's words rang anew when we learned the identity of the Vietnam War pilot whose remains had been interred in the Tomb of the Unknowns at Arlington National Cemetery.

No one ever got around to making a "Gettysburg Address" that would explain to us the purpose of our role in the Vietnam War. Yet throughout my reporting in that war, I found that the men and women who served there already knew their purpose.

We should never forget, or allow subsequent generations to forget, that whatever the government's purpose may have been in waging the Vietnam War, most of the American men and women who went believed they were fighting for freedom.

This reporter was honored to have covered America's warriors in Vietnam. I am proud to have known them, proud to have witnessed their odyssey in that green jungle hell.

They may have gone to the wrong war, but they went for

the right reasons: they believed in service to their country, and they believed in the cause of liberty.

Today, where the remains of Michael Blassie once rested in the Tomb of the Unknowns, there is an empty space.

For many Americans, the Vietnam War itself is like a space that can't be filled. As a nation, we strive to pay apt tribute to those who served and sacrificed. At the same time, we feel conflicting emotions: pride in our sons and daughters, dismay at the bloodshed, grief at the losses, anger at those who lied to us, frustration at the victory that history denied us.

Advances in forensic science now make it unlikely that another unknown warrior from Vietnam or any future war will ever rest in the Tomb at Arlington.

So how can America as a nation pay tribute to our men and women who gave that "last full measure of devotion"?

We may never find a way. But we must surely try.

The Chinese are still struggling to understand and obtain liberty. The Americans are still struggling to uphold it.

We have known terrible casualties in that struggle. But the cause was never sweeter.

And that's what we're celebrating.

Investigations by CBS News reporter Vince Gonzales led to the Pentagon's identification of Blassie's remains.

PROTECTING THE DREAM— AND THE PROTECTORS
July 15, 1998

In the aftermath of CNN's discredited report about the alleged use of lethal gas by U.S. forces in Laos, an old accusation against the press is being revived. It is the charge that the majority of American journalists are antimilitary.

It isn't true. Never has been. The fact is, and the record shows, American journalists as a whole are and have been over the years, decidedly promilitary. Foreign reporters and other international observers often accuse us of favoring our armed forces—and they're right.

We try not to show our bias, but it manifests itself almost every time U.S. military forces are deployed anywhere in the world.

This includes Vietnam. It's a myth that most American journalists in Vietnam didn't like the military, weren't pulling for America to win, and as a consequence "the media lost the war."

Some Americans, including some who fought valiantly in Vietnam, genuinely believe that myth. But others have viciously spread the myth for their own self-serving, often very partisan political purposes. The worst among these people were never in Vietnam, including some who went to great lengths to avoid going when it was most dangerous. Now, whenever it suits their purposes, they pose as experts.

This reporter reserves special scorn for such people.

Journalists are not blameless. We often bring the criticism upon ourselves, sometimes through carelessness, sometimes through arrogance, and yes, in at least a few cases, because a very few American journalists do have antimilitary biases.

All journalists make mistakes. That specifically includes myself. It also includes CNN, a basically good outfit that has admitted it created its own nightmare in that discredited report. However it happened, for whatever reasons, it was a mistake.

But there is now a concerted effort under way in some quarters to smear American journalists as a group because of that mistake.

Based on long personal experience with American military men and women, this reporter doubts that most rank-and-file members of our military services will sucker for this smear, for the same reason most of the general American public won't. They're too smart. They read, listen to, and watch the news.

Americans will judge us individually. And they'll do the same with our accusers—some politicians, including some self-described "conservatives"; and some people with admirable military service records. Americans will see that some of our accusers are sincere, while others are simply opportunists.

Americans will reason it out—just as they reasoned, for example, that it would be senseless and indecent to blame the whole Army for the atrocities committed at My Lai by one company.

However, some people are easily misled. And about this, we journalists need to be more careful, thoughtful, and more willing to admit our mistakes.

Sometimes we defend the fundamental truth of a story without acknowledging how it comes across—and that's a mistake. A story may be true, but still perceived as biased if the facts are not presented in full, with careful attention to context and perspective. And the *perception* of bias can be as damaging to a journalist's reputation as the *existence* of bias.

We must scrutinize our work—and others'—for bias, and then correct it. We must be on high alert for even the perception of bias.

Journalism is not an exact science. It is, even at its best, a crude art. To pretend otherwise makes us vulnerable to misconceptions, even smears, such as the present one.

In the land of the American dream, someone must protect the dreamers. Experienced journalists know this. And about this, most of us are biased—fiercely so.

ADOPTION
March 19, 1993

Modern medicine has come so far, yet attitudes sometimes lag behind. For all the improvements in fertility and medical technology, more and more of us now know childless couples who have become parents, not through test tube babies, but through adoption. So, after you've said, "Congratulations," what do you say next?

You'd be surprised what people *do* say. People who would never call women "girls," people who would never call an American Indian a "redskin," will let loose with some doozies.

So, without further ado, here are some of the most common—and the most inappropriate. Like this one: "Now that you've adopted you're probably going to get pregnant and have a child of your own."

Reality check: medically, it's not necessarily true. Morally . . . and legally . . . an adopted child is very much a child of your own. We're not talking about DNA here, we're talking about love. *Family,* not family *tree.*

Many people will refer to the adopted child's birth parents as "the real parents" . . . as in "Do you know who the real parents are?" The implication here is that the adoptive parents are somehow *unreal.*

Here's some context and perspective. What makes a real parent? Being responsible for a child's conception? Or being there for the child's first step, first word, comforting that child when sick, or reading the goodnight story?

Then there are the historical hurts and insults that manage to distort the role of *all* the parties involved in modern-day adoptions: the birth parents, the adoptive parents, and the child. How many times, in word and in print, have you heard the phrases "given up for adoption," "given away for adoption," or "put up for adoption"? Fact: the phrase "put up for adoption" refers to a practice in the last century, when they would round up the orphans in a city, bring them to a central place, and *literally* put them up for adoption.

Now, forget about what's politically correct, and just think about what is polite, sensitive, what *you* would want to hear if you were an adoptive parent. Tuck this information away. You never know when you might need it. In the meantime, if you're at a loss about what to say to adoptive parents . . . try "Mazel tov!"

> *The preceding essay was written by Paul Fischer, one of the writers of the* CBS Evening News. *Few broadcasts of* Dan Rather Reporting *ever provoked such an outburst of approval from our listeners.*

LEADING LIBRARIAN SAYS
RENEWAL IS OVERDUE
April 8, 1998

SAN ANTONIO, TEXAS—"One of the wonders of the twentieth century is America's public libraries. They are such a treasure, such an important part of what we, as a people, have become. The problem, and it's a growing one, is that Americans have come to take them for granted. I worry about what is to become of our libraries in the century ahead."

The speaker is the First Lady of Texas, Laura Bush, wife of Governor George W. Bush. A former public school teacher and librarian, she is speaking with your reporter inside San Antonio's magnificent new central public library.

One of the outstanding new architectural sites in the whole country, this is a six-story, chili-red building designed by the great Mexican architect Ricardo Legorreta. There is nothing quite like it, architecturally, anywhere in the United States.

Laura Welch Bush is here for the annual conference of the Texas Library Association.

She's fifty-one now, but doesn't look it. The mother of sixteen-year-old twins, she is trim, with a smashing smile and quiet grace befitting the librarian she was educated to be.

If her husband becomes the Republican presidential nominee in 2000, as many expect, she will be a formidable asset to him. She already is. As one Texan observed during the conference, "People may disagree with the politics of the Bush men, but you can't deny that they know how to pick their wives."

Mrs. Bush shares the Bush family's commitment to promoting literacy. And libraries are her passion.

"What America's libraries are to become in the twenty-first century, I have no idea," she is saying, referring to the technological advances that are causing a quiet revolution in libraries, catalogs, and collections worldwide. "But this much I do know: if libraries do not remain widely and substantially supported, we, our children, and our children's children will suffer: economically, intellectually, and spiritually.

"One reason this has been the 'American Century' has been the rapid development, early in this century, of public libraries."

And right she is. Although public libraries had been around for a while, it was early in this century that steel magnate Andrew Carnegie poured his considerable fortune into endowments for over 2,800 libraries throughout America and Britain.

Carnegie grew up poor: most institutions of learning had been closed to him as a boy. But he valued learning and wanted future generations to find an easier road to the kind of success he'd attained. Libraries, he believed, represented opportunities to read, learn, and grow.

By the 1930s, public libraries were the pride of America's towns and cities, large and small. These beautiful buildings were known as "Palaces of the People."

But several years ago, as "tax revolts" spread across the country, libraries became a favorite target of budget cutters.

Numbers of new libraries declined, acquisitions of new books fell, and preservation of old books became a luxury. Hours were cut back, sometimes drastically, so that some libraries were open only a few days a week.

Are we now seeing that trend in turnaround? Do San Antonio's new library, and Denver's recently remodeled one, represent a renaissance, a renewed emphasis on public libraries?

Laura Bush finds that a librarian's regard for silence can be politically useful: if she has any specific plans, she doesn't share them now. Instead, she smiles demurely and says, "I hope so."

But her bright blue eyes speak loudly. As the Internet bids to become King of the Information Age, as budgets shrink, too few Americans seem to care what happens to the Palaces of the People that are our libraries.

But Laura Bush is not among them.

THE W.N.B.A.
August 13, 1997

You may be surprised to learn that the big names in sports this summer aren't Mark Messier, Tiger Woods, or Hideki Irabu. No, they're more like Rebecca Lobo, Sheryl Swoopes, and Lisa Leslie.

For those who may not recognize them, these three female sports stars are top players in the W.N.B.A., the new professional women's basketball league, which began its inaugural season this June.

The Women's National Basketball Association is the sister league of the fifty-year-old National Basketball Association, and in the W.N.B.A.'s first season, eight charter teams have been split into two conferences. Over a twenty-eight-game, ten-week season, the teams are playing in major cities where N.B.A. teams are also located. The women's teams include the Houston Comets, the New York Liberty, the Charlotte Sting, and the Utah Starzz.

In building up the league, elite basketball players were recruited from around the world—many who have won college titles and Olympic medals. A few already have the attention of big advertisers, and can be seen in commercials promoting sneakers and sports drinks just the way their male counterparts do. And while women hoopsters may not be earning the same salaries as The Mailman or Shaq, they've been playing just as tough.

Not many know that professional women's basketball has a long history. Several attempts were made to establish leagues over the past few decades, but all ended quickly due to a general lack of support and financial backing.

Just last year, the American Basketball League, another professional women's league, got under way. Yet the A.B.L. remains nearly anonymous, and its games have won little notice. The W.N.B.A., on the other hand, is attempting to change women's athletics and their perception in popular culture at large. The league has had wide promotion with the help of national television coverage and major corporate sponsorships, in addition to the financial and marketing muscle of the N.B.A.

As the teams approach their first play-offs at the end of the month, crowds continue to fill arenas, and the televised games earn solid ratings. In the future, the W.N.B.A. aims to place a women's team in all twenty-nine N.B.A. cities. But for now, basketball fans—both men and women—have bestowed on the W.N.B.A. its own place in sports history.

Sakura Komiyama, associate producer of Dan Rather Reporting *and an invaluable member of our CBS News team, wrote the preceding essay.*

PLAY BALL?
April 9, 1996

This is ridiculous. I'm listening to and watching what is supposed to be the opening day of the baseball season at Yankee Stadium.

It is cold, rainy, even snowy. What in the world could they be thinking, the people who own and run baseball? I refer to this business of opening the season in March. Yes, the season was opened in *March*. Not at Yankee Stadium but in Seattle. And, the day after that, the Mets at Shea Stadium here in New York on, yes, another cold, wet day.

Baseball had that crazy strike and lockout last year. Just tore up the whole season. Greed is what did it. Greed of the owners, greed of the players. And a long-outdated antitrust exemption, allowed by Congress, serves to fuel, aid, and abet the greed.

Baseball was hurt, badly hurt, by that ill-advised lockout and strike. This reporter, a lifetime baseball enthusiast, actually swore off the sport at that time. Said he was through with baseball for the year, as a small protest. That would hardly be worth mentioning except that many other fans thought, said, and did the same thing.

Ah, but this year, this year was a new year. This year was going to be different. All was not forgiven the baseball moguls and their players, likewise destructive to the game. "But what the heck," we thought. We'd go back to the ballparks. And try to pick up where we left off, enjoying the game.

Who would have thought anybody in baseball would have been crazy enough to start the season in March? Baseball is a warm-weather game. Every schoolchild knows that warm weather doesn't come to most of the country until at least mid-April. At least.

So why did they do it? Money, of course. The owners want

to stretch the season from the cold of March right through the cold of late October, on into November if need be. More games, more money—especially more television money. But also more money for everything from tickets to parking to concessions.

Disgusting. There is no other word for it. But here it is. The Yankees are opening their season in the snow.

So baseball grinds on with its self-destructive ways. Nobody does anything about it. Nobody can do anything about it, at least nobody short of the owners and perhaps Congress.

What does it matter? Not much, maybe, in the big scheme of things. Except that baseball is so much a part of America. It adds so much to the spirit and fiber of the country, with its emphasis on individual skills united in the framework of a great team.

Too bad greed is killing it.

THE INTERNET: A NEWS REVOLUTION?

The following piece is an adaptation for this book of a speech I gave in various forms in late 1999. Obviously, the Internet is here big and here to stay. It's come on so fast that we have not always had the time to weigh the new challenges it confronts us with . . . until we find ourselves knee-deep in them. News is just one of the many ways the Internet is touching our lives, but it is the area I know best and the one that affects me the most. And I think we need to stop now and then and think about our headlong rush to embrace the new, if only so that we can be sure to grab on to it in the right way.

Something's been on my mind a lot lately, and it's not— you may be relieved to hear—the approach of the millennium.

Though it *is* about the new and the future . . . and how we might make peace between what is new and what has come to be regarded as the traditional way of doing things.

I've been thinking about the Internet and the news, and the way the news is reported. And how the Internet is likely to affect that . . . how it is already affecting the news.

Now I know you may be thinking, "Whoa, hold on a minute, Rather, you're from *television*. . . . You're going to come at us as the voice of *tradition*?"

Funny, isn't it, how innovation eventually makes traditionalists of us all. . . . And even the Internet has gone from being the latest catchphrase and buzzword to being a basic fact of life . . . in what can only be regarded as a mind-spinningly short step of time.

I said that I wasn't going to talk about the turn of the millennium or the century, but I think it's worth reflecting a moment on the pace of change in the twentieth century. How, since the dawn of civilization, man's speed limit was a horse at full gallop—tens of thousands of years got us forty miles an hour, tops, sustainable for only a few minutes at a time.

Yet in the not much more than a hundred years since the invention of the locomotive—in a couple of lifetimes— we've gone from galloping to riding the rails to shooting ourselves into space at more than twenty times the speed of sound.

And we might recall, just three short years ago, the almost poignant spectacle of my friend Bob Dole trying to give his campaign's web address during his first debate with Bill Clinton in the 1996 presidential campaign. How new this all seemed—to many of us—even then. And it was clear from Dole's delivery that, great American though he is, back then he didn't know a dot-com or dot-org from a polka dot.

It was during our CBS News coverage of that same presidential debate that I had one of my own early impressions of the Internet's power. No sooner had I given our viewers the CBS web address for our on-line coverage of the debate than upwards of a million people logged on . . . more or less, our computer people told me, at once.

We have, in this American century, found ourselves in the paradoxical situation of becoming accustomed to change. And it's happening more, and faster, than ever.

The wondrous speed of change can excite and frighten . . . and greater men than I have commented on change as it relates to media.

One, whom I respect very much, noted, "The speed of communication is wondrous to behold," but "It is also true that speed can multiply the distribution of information that we know to be untrue."

Another observed that "[It] is the first truly democratic culture—the first culture available to everyone and entirely governed by what the people want. The most terrifying thing is what the people *do* want."

And pithy—and perceptive in its way—was this line: "It's like indoor plumbing—it didn't change people's habits. It just kept them inside the house."

Would it surprise you to hear that these comments are decades old? Alfred Hitchcock spoke those last words, and the first—about the speed of communication multiplying untruths—belong to Edward R. Murrow, the father of broadcast journalism.

They're all talking about not the Internet but television . . . which in *its* infancy was greeted with the same mix of handwringing and hallelujahs that the Internet stirs up today.

And, some fifty-odd years down the road, you know what? Both the optimists and the pessimists have turned out to be right . . . our critics' worst fears have been borne out and so have some of our dreamers' greatest hopes for the medium.

At our best, those of us in television news have given the word "journalist" every bit as much weight in the equation as the word "broadcast."

And, at our worst, we have favored image over informed

coverage, anecdote over truth, narrative simplicity over real complexity.

Our record in television is mixed . . . and the medium's history is still very much a work in progress. I say this all by way of looking again at the Internet, and television, and the news: where they might all come together in a way that has a chance of doing us some good and where we might be able to learn from the lessons television has taught us.

But first we should acknowledge that the Internet will also provide its own lessons . . . the same way that television did to its pioneers. It took a while for these dedicated folks to realize that their little box with pictures was more than a souped-up radio, that television's visual aspect could be harnessed not only to illustrate a story, but to *tell* a story in a new and unique way.

The Internet, new form of mass communication that it is, carries its own unique potential . . . and perils. And we're still, most of us, thinking of the Internet in terms of what has come before it.

Just as many of us did when we first used a word processor: until you learned to approach this new vehicle for expression on its own terms, all you had was a glorified typewriter with a fat instruction manual.

I should add that—make no mistake—I am no great expert on the Internet. But what I'm talking about today has been percolating in the back of my mind since the whole affair with the Drudge report breaking several of the more tawdry aspects of the Lewinsky story . . . and I've had the chance to think about the Internet and the news again recently, as CBS News launched a new Internet partnership called HealthWatch.

So I come to the issue from the point of view of someone who cares deeply about the news, and as one—might as well admit it—who inevitably sees the Internet through the lens of television.

We can see right away that a big difference between television and the Internet is that the Internet takes a step through that "fourth wall" to be . . . interactive.

For the news, I think, this affords an opportunity to not only report to the viewing public but to truly reach them with the information they need to know . . . and the information our democracy needs the people to know. It's a lesson known to every college professor, to every teacher—or, at least, the really good ones: if you want your students to retain what you say, don't just lean against a lectern and let pearls of wisdom drop from your lips . . . engage them, question them.

Consider how much better you would remember the content of the evening news if you were, in some way, a participant.

The future . . . if we dare look into its murky cloud . . . is taking us toward a marriage of television and the Internet. It may not be very long at all before any distinction between the two belongs distinctly to the past. We now have streaming video on-line, webcasts, and partnerships between television news programs and websites, like the one at CBS that got me thinking about all this.

It's an exciting development in many ways, this move toward interactivity—particularly in the news, and particularly if we remember that no amount of technological wizardry can take the place of quality content.

But there are certain places where I think we need to stand guard at the dawn of this revolution. Because even if we take the Internet on its own terms, we can't ignore what our experience tells us about the dangers we may face in putting and getting news on-line. We have, in fact, already seen evidence of some of these.

My esteemed predecessor in the anchor chair, my good friend Walter Cronkite, came out and said it straight, no chaser, that the Internet could be "a frightful danger to all of us." By "all of us," he meant *all* of us . . . but he also meant, specifically, all of us whose lifeblood is the news.

Now, if we learned anything watching Walter all those

years, it was that, yes, he'd give it to you straight . . . and he also wasn't given to overstatement.

What provoked this particular dire statement was the flap around former Kennedy Press Secretary Pierre Salinger's claim to have proof that TWA's Flight 800 was shot down by a missile fired from an American naval vessel. Salinger's "proof" turned out to be a bogus document he'd found on the Internet . . . an unfortunate embarrassment for an esteemed public figure. It was an even greater embarrassment to those who ran with the story.

I don't say this to pick on Pierre, but he had fallen prey to one of the pitfalls of information . . . information of uncertain origin . . . found on the Internet: its reliability. Or, in this case, its lack thereof.

Common sense could take us a long way in avoiding this sort of trap. Because the reliability snare is one the Internet shares with all public forums—when everyone's talking, you can't always believe what you hear. Of course, we should always practice a healthy skepticism, no matter what our source of information. But certain news programs, certain newspapers, certain journals have a demonstrable record of truth telling, of accuracy in their reporting. I pretend no false modesty in saying that I hold CBS News high—very high—in this regard. And, of course, I also recognize the records of our network competitors in this. . . . We've all built reliability through years of hard work.

The thing about the Internet is, just about anyone can set up a website that looks like, has the feel of, news organs we've learned to trust. Broadcasting the news, especially, has traditionally been an expensive proposition. And if you don't cast the die for truth telling from the start, if you don't burnish it with every story you do, then you, your network, your newspaper, your magazine . . . are throwing that capital investment right down the drain. Once caught in a lie, or in a pattern of error, you will be tuned out.

As journalists we have an ethical code. This is important to us. Important enough that reporters have given their very lives to get you the real story. But even if it were not, it would still obtain in large part because to do it any other way would simply be bad business. And even if the news itself is not a business—television is, publishing is.

On the Net, a legitimate look doesn't always assure that journalism is being practiced. A voice crying in the wilderness of the Internet may not even care if you believe it tomorrow, let alone the next day. The accountability . . . the *reliability* . . . is not, until tested, always there.

The Internet as town square—a gossiping, teeming hub of communication—is undeniably part of its excitement. But those of us who do news and care about doing it right must remember that we are bound to separate gossip from fact.

We might hope that news people in established media might tame this impulse on the Internet, at least aid in separating the gossip—the "paranews"—from the news. But we have reason to fear that the trend is working the other way.

Certain precincts of the Internet threaten to be another place—like the supermarket tabloids—where legitimate news organs can point and say, "Hey, *we're* not saying this our-selves, but we're going to take a look at what *they're* reporting, just so you know. . . ." We need to be closing these back doors for gossip to find its way into the news, not opening more. We ought to make it crystal clear that, if you feed from the bottom, you're not going to be kosher.

If gossip has found its way onto the news through a back door, at the front door, traditionally, is the gatekeeper . . . the managing editor. This is my title at the *CBS Evening News*—anchor and managing editor. It is no stretch to say that this is what we call a big responsibility.

The managing editor of a newspaper, of a news broadcast has the bottom-line task of separating the wheat from the chaff, using hard-won professional judgment to separate real information from MISinformation: *this* item gets in; this *may* get in, but only if there's nothing more pressing; this other item may get in, but only if we can corroborate it with another source; and this thing, over here, NO, it does not get in . . . it is unsubstantiated, or fluff, or too narrowly serves a specific interest or, innocently enough, is simply not that important.

With the Internet now comes the potential to act as one's own managing editor, one's own gatekeeper. . . . It's an exciting possibility, but one we must learn to use wisely.

Because now you can get news from more or less traditional sources, but just the news you say you want.

This doesn't seem so bad, on its face. Isn't this, after all, a big part of what the Internet is all about? Tailoring an experience to an interest, to a personal schedule . . . bringing the like-minded from across the country—around the world, at all hours—together in cyberspace?

Well, it's a double-edged sword. And we ought to recognize that this trend could contribute to the balkanization of our society . . . of our lives, public and private. In a way, sure, the Internet is the realized ideal of the town meeting . . . but no one foresaw a town meeting where you wouldn't have to listen to everyone in the room.

And while winnowing the information gusher to a more manageable, personalized stream makes perfect sense for specific areas of interest, we ought to be careful that we don't all fall into the habit of looking through the whole world *only* through this sort of hyperfocused lens.

In America, where informed citizens are a necessity, the journalists and managing editors among us have understood— not always perfectly, but almost always in good faith—our role in fostering a common share of knowledge and understanding.

With the enormous challenges we're likely to face in our weeks and months and years ahead, we can afford now less than ever to become wrapped in self-configured cocoons of information.

Perhaps the time has come for us to rediscover the value of

shared experience, of shared information, of some common, daily element that keeps our hand in public life. The stakes are simply too high for us to fold on this. For the past fifty years, television news has played this role of the public square—for better or worse—and it looks as if the Internet will play the role in some way in the future, with or without television. But we must make a conscious decision that we want to maintain a common society within the structures of the new media. Or we risk walking and talking past each other, with virtual blinders on . . . the great debates of our time monopolized by those with only the greatest personal or financial stake in their outcome . . . and all before we know it.

THE AIDS METAPHOR IN
BEAUTY AND THE BEAST
March 22, 1992

This essay began as one of my rare attempts at cultural criticism—not hard-news reporting. But the morning the essay ran in the Los Angeles Times, *I started getting telephone calls from people high and low at Disney, all asking the same question: "How did you find out?" My experience covering the Watergate crimes and cover-ups told me: these weren't questions, they were* confirmations. *I wasn't speculating, I was right.*

Yet rather than take credit for what remains Hollywood's most successful, and most eloquent, statement on the AIDS epidemic, Disney executives didn't want to be pinned down. Michael Eisner, the chairman of Disney, phoned me to let me know that AIDS was one of "several modern-day plagues" that "might be symbolized" by the Beast's curse. (Folks farther down Disney's establishment

*later admitted the AIDS symbolism quite freely to me—
but not for attribution.) At the time, Eisner couldn't
know that Disney would be boycotted five years later by
the Southern Baptist Convention for its "antifamily" policies—that is, for the company's tolerant attitudes toward homosexual employees and customers.*

In the end, I was convinced that Beauty and the Beast
*was, as the character Mrs. Potts sings, a "tale as old as
time"—and as current as today's headlines.*

*And in the years since this Disney release, Holly-
wood's near silence on one of the great plagues of our
time has continued. . . . Again, aside from art-house and
movie-of-the-week offerings, there has been only a small
group of characters with AIDS, much less movies focusing on the subject.* Philadelphia *(1993), starring Tom
Hanks, is just about the only one that comes to the mind
of your reporter.*

I am not generally known for being a movie critic. Quite
the contrary. (Although just the other day Roger Ebert took
me to task for my reviews of Oliver Stone's *J.F.K.* This was a
little puzzling, since I hadn't written any reviews of Oliver
Stone's *J.F.K.*, but perhaps Mr. Ebert had me mistaken for
Gene Siskel, who works the morning shift at CBS News. Gene
and I have both been known to wear sweaters: the confusion
was bound to arise eventually.)

But I do enjoy movies (*J.F.K.* included), and like anybody
else who plunks down his money for a ticket and a tub of
popcorn, I've got my opinions and my interpretations.

Opinions: I like Kathleen Turner and I think Sissy Spacek
is one of Texas's most valuable exports.

Interpretations: the news colors every picture ever made in
Hollywood. You know that already. If Ginger Rogers is up to
her permanent wave in sequins and feathers, it's only because
America doesn't want to look at more breadlines. If Michael
J. Pollard nearly becomes a matinee idol, it's because America

is rebelling against the Official Line, even the Official Definition of Matinee Idols. If Kevin Costner says that John Kennedy was shot to keep us in Vietnam, it's because America wants a way to make sense out of two painful episodes of the sixties.

I was thinking about this the other evening when I saw Disney's *Beauty and the Beast*. It's a great show: funny, sentimental, great songs and a multitalented cast of voices and drawings. The heronine, Belle, is spunky enough that I'm pretty sure she's got Texas roots, no matter what they tell me about her being French. (I do want to know why she's so much smaller when she's riding her horse, Philippe, than when she's standing next to him. Walt wouldn't have tolerated those changing proportions.)

But I kept thinking about the Beast.

The Beast is—just in case you've been in Frontierland and haven't heard the story yet—a prince who has a limited amount of time (the life span of a single flower) to find true love and break the spell that's made him a gruesome monster. He's cast out by society, even tracked down and attacked by an angry mob, and his only companions are also under the same spell. He's so desperate to break the spell, to rescue himself and his friends, that he can't control his temper—he smashes things, frightens people—and winds up even harder to love. He can't help himself.

You really feel for the guy. He reminds you of the hopeless klutz you were the first time you fell in love, always saying the wrong things, stepping on toes, trampling the flowers. And he reminded me of somebody else, somebody I've seen over and over as I've covered the news in the last decade: a Person With AIDS.

The more I think about it, the more sense it makes. Think of the spell as AIDS, with the same arbitrary and harshly abbreviated limitations on time, and you feel the Beast's loneliness and desperation a little more deeply. He's just a guy trying as hard as he can to find a little meaning—a little love, a little *beauty*—while he's still got a little life left.

After all, if the curse is just a curse, do the fundamental things apply? Why be so worried about breaking the spell when the Beast and his buddies can stay forever in that terrific castle, with nobody to bother them (the bully Gaston wouldn't ever have found them had it not been for the Beast's carelessness). Since Mrs. Potts, Lumière, Coggsworth, and Chip are handy household items, they don't need to worry about jobs—or about dying, for that matter, as long as they don't get broken. They're already together, so this isn't like Dorothy in *The Wizard of Oz,* who really must get back to her family.

What's the problem?

The folks at Disney tell me that *Beauty and the Beast* was well under way before lyricist and executive producer Howard Ashman tested HIV-positive, and long before Ashman died of AIDS. They say it isn't autobiographical. Instead, it's part of Ashman's living legacy—one that also includes wonderful words in shows like *The Little Mermaid* and *The Little Shop of Horrors,* and some of the lyrics in the forthcoming *Aladdin.*

But think what that legacy means if my interpretation is valid.

Susan Sontag has said that every society picks an illness and assigns it meaning—people force diseases to say something about themselves. *Illness as Metaphor* is the title of her book, and it's a tidy phrase, too. In the nineteenth century, we were obsessed by tuberculosis (think of Greta Garbo in *Camille*), and for most of the twentieth century, we were fascinated by cancer (think of Ali McGraw in *Love Story*). So far, there hasn't been a drama about AIDS with that kind of mainstream success. Writers and producers try, but so far we've seen only some movies-of-the-week and some art-house films: *An Early Frost* or *A Virus Knows No Morals. Longtime Companion* is as close to the mainstream as anybody's gotten without getting commercial.

Say that the AIDS metaphor is just one way, a valid way, of looking at *Beauty and the Beast.* That means that millions of Americans, most of them children, are looking at a Person

With AIDS with a new kind of compassion. We're crying for him when he's sad, cheering for him when he wins. You can hope that huge audiences would feel the same way about a real Person With AIDS, Kaposi's sarcoma lesions, and all the most visible symptoms of the full-blown illness. You can expect that we'd feel pity. But can you possibly imagine that we'd *identify* with him?

Actually, now that we know how to identify with the Beast, maybe we *can* identify with People With AIDS.

That's an achievement that makes something like a nomination for the Best Picture Academy Award look insignificant.

Because it means a new kind of hope, too. The People With AIDS that I've met, the folks I've talked with, all say that other people's attitudes are the biggest problems. Those are the attitudes that slow up the approval (or jack up the prices) for medications which might help, that immobilize political action, that impede education and prevention, that retract a helping hand, that deny a kind word.

Can you honestly say you'd turn down the Beast if he came to you for help?

If people's attitudes about People With AIDS can change, then *living* with AIDS will change. For the better.

Maybe I'm more wrong in trying to find social significance in a Disney cartoon than I am in trying to write movie criticism. But *Beauty and the Beast* has given me a lot to think about—about love, about loneliness, about compassion and fear. And about hope.

I give it two thumbs up.

Chapter 2

FOREIGN POLICIES,
GLOBAL
PERSPECTIVES

CHINA, AMERICA, AND THE FUTURE
April 29, 1998

Wang Dan, one of the great heroes of Tiananmen Square, sits uncomfortably for the interview. His eyes dart, and he shifts in his chair. And why wouldn't he feel unsettled?

He is only a few days out of a Chinese prison, whisked to Detroit and then to New York. He is a stranger in a strange land, where he does not speak the language and is suddenly inundated by attention—and responsibilities.

Mainly he feels a responsibility to speak for those Chinese who cannot speak for themselves, for fear that they, too, will be thrown in prison.

They are the Chinese who yearn for freedom and democracy, including representative government. They are the Chinese who do not agree with the old-line, hard-line Communists who still rule their country and its 1.3 billion people.

Wang Dan is twenty-nine now. Your reporter first met him and last saw him when he was twenty, in the cauldron that was Beijing's Tiananmen Square in 1989. He was a history student then, one of China's best and brightest. He and a few other student leaders were gambling everything on a bold challenge to China's repressive rulers.

They lost. Their movement swelled and crested just short of forcing dramatic change. It was crushed by tanks and troops. Wang Dan survived but became a wanted fugitive, hiding in southern China.

In another act of courage, he returned to Beijing late in 1989. Refusing to remain silent, he was imprisoned. He was released in 1993, then jailed again in 1995.

His release this spring has been widely interpreted as a public relations move by the Chinese government in advance of President Clinton's scheduled trip to China in late June.

Wang Dan told me that China's leaders have bluffed President Clinton and American business leaders into believing they must choose between seeking profits and lobbying for human rights. "It doesn't have to be one or the other," he says. "America can have both, do both."

On the human rights front, China is regularly cited for growing abuse of Christians, although the American government consistently downplays or ignores the charges. Church leaders and services are strictly regulated by the Chinese Communist party. Christians who refuse to adhere to government regulations worship in outlawed "underground" churches, where risk of discovery and punishment is constant.

"I have Christian friends who are monitored, observed, followed, even beaten," Wang Dan says. "I once issued a call on behalf of a Christian because he just wanted to persist in his beliefs, and he [had been] locked up and beaten."

Is it China's destiny to become a combined economic and military superpower in the twenty-first century? I asked this brilliant student of history.

"China is now at a critical juncture. For the past twenty years, it's basically been walking on one leg, because they've been open about economic reform but not about political reforms. In the twenty-first century, if they keep going in the same way, then China may go down the road to chaos.

"Because political reforms are not developed adequately, all of those who have been on the short end of economic reforms have no way to express their dissatisfaction. They may be looking increasingly for outlets for their discontent, and this could easily lead to chaos in the society."

China is still ruled by men, he says as he leaves. Until and unless it builds a rule of law based on the principles of democracy, he says, China cannot become the rich and stable society for which its people yearn.

In 1999, the People's Republic of China celebrated its fiftieth birthday, and the world marked the tenth anniversary of the events in Tiananmen Square. Though China's economy continues to gather steam, the evidence for the advance of political freedom was not great—the state rounded up large numbers of dissidents in preparation for the fiftieth anniversary celebration in October.

YELTSIN RESHUFFLES THE DECK
March 25, 1998

Boris Yeltsin's reshuffling of his cabinet shouldn't be brushed off by Americans. Russia and the reforms Yeltsin has led are in trouble.

And when there are political and economic troubles in Russia, Main Street USA must care. Here's why:

• The world can know little peace or prosperity without stability in Russia. This is a major lesson of twentieth-century history. Even in this, the post–Soviet era, that country still controls too much of the earth's surface and too many of its natural resources to be irrelevant. Moreover, Russia is still the only country other than the United States with a large arsenal of dependable intercontinental nuclear missiles.

• As China drives determinedly to become both an economic and military superpower, Russia is a key counterbalance. It will remain so far into the twenty-first century.

In thinking about this, it is important to remind ourselves that there are vast differences between the two largest cities,

Moscow and St. Petersburg, and the rest of Russia. An estimated 80 percent of real incomes is centered in those two urban centers.

"In the vast countryside that is Mother Russia, the nation is slowly lurching back to the nineteenth century," says Princeton professor and Russian expert Stephen Cohen. (Echoing his statement, figures released this week confirm the resurgence of tuberculosis, scourge of the nineteenth century, in Russia today.) "The Russian economy is much worse than most Americans have been led to believe," Cohen says.

Yeltsin is sixty-seven, ailing, and desperately trying to hold on to power and keep alive the economic and political changes he installed since 1991.

This won't be easy. Yeltsin emphasized this to me the last time I talked to him privately a few years ago.

"Dramatic change is always difficult," he said, adding, "especially in a country as large, as diverse, and as complicated as mine."

As he said this, he gestured with his crippled left hand. It was mangled in a grenade accident when he was a boy.

We talked in one of his private offices outside the Kremlin. He mostly talked optimistically about Russia's future as a major world power and as a friend of the United States.

This is why, regardless of how hard it may be to love or understand Yeltsin, Americans must pull for him to stay sober, stay alive, and continue to lead.

(Note: Russian Foreign Minister Yevgeny Primakov, the wily, pro-Saddam survivor of whom this reporter has written recently, seems to have survived Yeltsin's cabinet shake-up. Beaming, he told U.S. Secretary of State Madeleine Albright, "I have disappointing news for you: I haven't been fired.")

Primakov survived Yeltsin's March 1998 shake-up, and was even tapped by the president to succeed Sergei Kiriyenko as prime minister in September. By the following May, however, he was replaced himself, by Sergei

Stepashin. Yeltsin didn't stop there. In August 1999, desperate to anoint his own successor, he replaced Stepashin with Vladimir V. Putin. And for his final shake up, Yeltsin himself stepped down on New Year's Eve 1999, handing the reins to Putin.

STRAIGHT TALK ON IRAQ
February 28, 1998

President Clinton could use a little wise counsel on Iraq and Middle Eastern affairs these days. Too bad he hasn't taken the time to talk to Fouad Ajami.

One of the smartest, most experienced, and wisest Americans about the Middle East, Ajami teaches just down the road from the White House, at Johns Hopkins University in Washington.

An intense, bearded man in his fifties, with the compact build and quick moves of a scatback, Ajami was born in Lebanon. Educated by Middle Eastern scholars, he has traveled the region extensively for a lifetime. His new book, *The Dream Palace of the Arabs* (published last year by Pantheon Books), proves once again how clear-eyed and well considered his expertise is.

He views Saddam Hussein as "a jackal, cunning and vicious," an opponent tailormade to give "idealistic and decent-intending Americans such as Bill Clinton, Madeleine Albright, and Sandy Berger fits—and nothing but misery."

This also explains, says Ajami, why Saddam suckered Ronald Reagan and George Bush so effectively, for so much, for so long.

"Psychologically and politically, Saddam has outmaneuvered American policy makers. Time after time, he has had

America playing his game, dancing his tune. And so it is again now. In the land of Saddam Hussein, we're playing by his rules. He brings us to the brink, then suddenly backs away from the brink as he gains his advantages.

"He has worked his way back into considerable influence in his neighborhood," Ajami says, and in regaining respect among Arabs, "he has undermined the American case for sanctions."

Ajami points to a number of American decisions that he believes made the sanctions less effective anyway.

"Bush allowed him to keep his helicopter forces and the best of his Republican Guard. Clinton has allowed him to rebuild alliances with Russia and France—and allowed him to more than double the amount of money he can gain from selling oil. It's gone up from two billion dollars every six months to five billion dollars every six months. So now Saddam's on a roll," Ajami says. "He's eroding the case for sanctions and underlining the isolation of American power in the Middle East as a whole."

Ajami is also scathing on the role of the Republican congressional leadership in contributing to Saddam's comeback. Senate Majority Leader Trent Lott and House Speaker Newt Gingrich have been "missing in action," he says, when it comes to courage and conviction in crafting effective opposition to Saddam. "They criticize Clinton, but what are their ideas? They don't seem to have any to which they are willing to commit fully."

Ajami says that, in spite of tough talk from Democrats and Republicans in Congress and in the White House, fear has prevailed. President Bush feared that, after Saddam, Iraq would be fragmented and vulnerable to an Iranian takeover. President Clinton shared this fear, for much of his presidency.

The result? Plenty of people talk about removing Saddam from power, but nobody takes decisive action.

Even the American people have been reluctant to commit to getting Saddam out. "Saddam knows that," Ajami says.

"Saddam was glued to his television, watching the spectacle of Columbus, Ohio, the great American heartland, rejecting even the Clinton policy of threatening Saddam with force."

To Saddam, the Columbus "town-hall meeting" (see page 140) was "affirmation and reassurance that once again he would survive, and move to greater influence in his neighborhood by playing hard and tough. He remains alive and well, free to continue working his strategy of cheat and retreat, then cheat again."

This is Professor Ajami's analysis. And it is the kind of straight talk one wonders whether the President ever hears.

SADDAM'S INFLUENTIAL ASSOCIATE
February 11, 1998

Having recently been in a room with Saddam Hussein, a foreign diplomat tells me:

"Saddam is tightly focused and, as always, supremely *determined*. He's among the most insular of leaders. He knows little of the outside world, especially the West. What little he does know of the West, has come to him filtered through the Russian foreign minister, Yevgeny Primakov."

Primakov is a longtime friend of Saddam. With Russian President Boris Yeltsin ailing and failing, Primakov is widely acknowledged to be making Moscow's decisions about Iraq. His views surely provoked Yeltsin's outburst last week—that U.S. action against Iraq might lead to World War III.

Your reporter has met Primakov several times. He loves his own power and is clearly driven by dreams of returning Russia to its glory days of empire. He was a true believer in communism, served for many years as a Soviet spy, and is believed to resent the U.S. intensely.

Many analysts believe that Primakov aims to join Russia, China, France, and Iraq in a loose alliance to counterbalance American power, especially in the Persian Gulf and Caspian Sea.

He's known to have helped supply Iraq with Russian weapons for years, and was a mentor to Saddam in his drive for preeminence around the Persian Gulf. Today Primakov holds oil interests that stand to reward him—and Saddam—personally when the embargo against Iraq is finally lifted.

No one outside Iraq, and few if any inside, is believed to have more influence with Saddam than Primakov in military and diplomatic decisions.

According to the foreign diplomat who recently saw Saddam, the Iraqi president "now believes that in one important way, *he* won the Gulf War. That is, he took America's best shot and survived. He is absolutely convinced that he can do so again.

"He believes that if the U.S. attacks again—and he thinks it will—he will again survive. And that in so doing, he will achieve another 'victory.' This may strike many as crazy, but that's what he thinks."

Your reporter thinks back to 1990 and a night alone in Baghdad with Saddam. With something like a smirk, he told me: "You Americans can't take the blood."

At the time, I believed he meant that the U.S. wouldn't attack. About that, he was wrong. Yet, in another sense, he was right: President George Bush called a halt to the successful assault after only a hundred hours of ground combat. Saddam survived with sufficient military force to maintain himself in power indefinitely.

Now, Saddam seems to be saying again, "You Americans can't take the blood." For the new air attacks being planned, Saddam can guarantee high civilian casualties. Once pictures of the devastation are disseminated worldwide, Saddam probably figures, the attack plan will be shortened, America will be condemned, and he, Saddam Hussein, will remain in power, "victorious" again.

Several countries' diplomats say Primakov is counseling

Saddam that if he gives the President a decent out, Bill Clinton will take it. This was his counsel in November 1997, and it worked—in a deal Primakov brokered. He's now trying for an encore.

The U.S. plan still calls for attacks, if there are to be any, to begin this month. But there are already indications from Washington that President Clinton is, at a minimum, having serious second thoughts about ordering a new attack. Private briefings for reporters have begun to emphasize diplomacy instead of aerial assaults.

Primakov and Saddam are in constant contact. Two cunning survivors scheming to survive yet again.

If they go down, they go down together. You can bet they both believe they'll make it through, somehow, and go on to their version of greater glory.

Saddam and Primakov both survived the crisis: President Clinton was offered what he believed to be a decent out, and he took it. At the time of this revision, however, a low-key bombing campaign against Iraq has been going on for months. Saddam is as entrenched as ever in leadership of Iraq. And though Primakov is no longer in the Russian government, he is now a candidate for the Russian presidency in 2000 . . . which will be decided just before this edition comes out.

CUBA'S NATIONAL PASTIME ISN'T POLITICS OR RELIGION
January 21, 1998

When Pope John Paul II made his visit to Cuba in January 1998, we found the island nation aflurry with preparations, yet curiously restrained. We soon found out the reason. Cuban President Fidel Castro had only conceded freedom of religion as a right a few years before, shortly after the demise of the Soviet Union; and after years of discouragement, oppression, and even violent repression of any religious activity, many Cubans were still wary of openly professing their faith in God. The Pope's visit was exciting, they told us, because this Pope is such a historic figure, not because they viewed him as a spiritual leader.

Significantly, although Castro had officially permitted the posting of welcoming banners and other activities pertaining to the Pope's visit, notification of that permission didn't reach all the party bosses in all the provinces: throughout our stay we heard reports of posters torn down and citizens punished, and we heard wildly conflicting interpretations of exactly how many Cubans were invited or expected to attend the four masses John Paul II would ultimately preach. Would they be permitted to cheer the Pope when he arrived? And, if the Cubans did attend a mass, would they be permitted to take communion, to kneel, to pray?

Churchgoing is still a novel idea in Castro's Cuba: mostly it is the very, very elderly who go to church regularly. One sunny Sunday, we found a group of small-town Cubans enthusiastically performing what they considered to be their holiest rites—that had nothing to do with Catholicism.

HAVANA—Come with me to the Cuba beyond Havana. Travel the two-lane blacktop thirty miles southwest of Castro's capital. Then turn onto the dirt road that leads to Vereda Nueva. This old farming town is typical of the real heart of Cuba, the countryside.

It's late of a Sunday morning. Everybody who is anybody is at the ballpark. Men, woman, and children—150, maybe

200 of them. We're told the town has an official population of over 4,000, If there are anywhere near 4,000 people actually living in this town, then I'm a left-handed shortstop.

This much I know: almost everything and everybody *moving* outdoors this Sunday morning is at the baseball game.

The playing field is a converted cow pasture. The backstop is chicken wire. There's barbed wire around the perimeter, where goats and a mule graze. The outfield is bounded by a combination picket and smooth wire fence.

It's big: 330 feet down the left-field line, 300 down the right, 390 to dead center.

Even in a country as poor as Cuba, great care—and some money—went into the construction of dugouts and stands. Now they're falling apart. The stands are slab concrete, painted in yellow and blue pastels, with a graceful roof of concrete and peeling plaster. There's a lemonade stand at one end, a hand water pump at the other, with privies out back.

Today's game pits the Grapefruit Pickers against the Dairy Workers. It's an amateur league, but nobody in the majors takes the game more seriously, plays it harder or with more savvy.

They execute the hit and run, the run and hit, and the double steal. They work a perfect suicide squeeze, and a timing pickoff at second base. All by the sixth inning.

In the seventh, with the score tied and two outs, the Dairy team has runners at first and third. For the second time in the inning, the Fruit Pickers' manager visits his pitcher on the mound. But he doesn't pull him. As the manager begins sauntering back to the dugout, the umpire reminds him of the rule: second trip to the mound in one inning, you must change pitchers.

An argument erupts into a near brawl, as both benches empty onto the field. The ump—of course—prevails. The Pickers replace their middle-aged and stocky sidearm sinker-ball ace with a stringbean, heat-throwing kid.

As the boy takes his warm-up pitches on the mound, one

of the Pickers fans tells me the Spanish equivalent of "this kid pitches so hard, he could throw a marshmallow through a locomotive."

Maybe so. But he's wild. He walks the first batter he faces on five pitches, loading the bases. His manager doesn't hesitate. He's out of the dugout like a man shot from a cannon. And he yanks the young'un.

Out of the shadows of the bullpen off the left-field foul line comes a stubble-bearded man of at least forty. He doesn't throw hard but he throws true. Strikeout. Swinging. Breaking ball. Low and away.

But his Pickers eventually lose. On a bottom of the ninth, two-out close play at the plate, the Milkmen score the winning run from second base with a ground-ball single through the right side.

Baseball as it was meant to be.

The husband of a local schoolteacher is watching the game. He's just bought some roasted peanuts in a slender paper cone. "In this area," he tells a stranger, "there are many *creyentes,* people who believe [in God]." He munches thoughtfully, then adds, "But there are many more people who believe in baseball."

CASTRO HEARS THE CLOCK
January 13, 1998

Of course the papal visit didn't turn out to be the public relations bonanza President Castro hoped. Within an hour of John Paul II's arrival in Havana, the American news organizations were packing their bags and heading for Washington, D.C., to swarm all over what, according to initial reports, was a scandal so huge that the Clinton presidency's expected life-span could be measured in days, not years. (I am more relieved than proud to report that, of the "big three" anchors, I was first to arrive and last to leave Cuba.)

The story we found turned out to be considerably less clear-cut and fast-moving; after three or four days of whirlwind, the charges against the President drifted into the usual Washington doldrums of countercharges and drawn-out investigations.

For his part, Castro, wily public relations expert that he is, must have been hopping mad. Well aware that his own personality is often the whole show where Cuba's PR is concerned, Castro had deliberately held back on granting so much as a press appearance—claiming he didn't want to upstage the Pope, teasing the entire foreign press corps with the promise of an appearance at the Habana Libre Hotel on the eve of the Pope's arrival, but then failing to show up and never confirming any of the numerous interview requests he'd received from every news organization, including my own.

Would he have done things differently if he thought he might have been able to hold the interest of the American networks? I'd bet on it.

I had last seen Castro nearly two years before. Cuba was crumbling without the props of the Soviet Union to support it. But what interested me most was the realization that Castro might be crumbling, too.

Fidel Castro's step is not as sure as it once was. Getting off a helicopter, the Cuban dictator is unsteady, and two soldiers take him by the forearms and guide him down the three short steps to level ground.

He seems softer, perhaps even a bit puffy. His baseball player's arms hang in his sleeves.

He has given up his trademark cigars—not for reasons of his own health, he insists, but to oblige his younger associates, one of whom is said to be asthmatic.

You can no longer bet that every speech will run seven or eight hours—per day—over a period of days. And the all-night talkathons with visitors are less common now. The commandante often packs it in early these days.

This reporter has been covering Fidel Castro for many years, and my first interview with him took place almost a quarter-century ago. It would be absurd to expect him to defy the passage of time. And yet, on my last meeting with him, a few months before his seventieth birthday in 1996, I was struck by how suddenly age had caught up with him.

Many Americans would prefer not to be reminded of it, but endurance seems to be one of Castro's special skills. Castro has outlasted every U.S. President who vowed to turn him out since 1959. Castro clearly hopes to outlast John Paul II, the famously anti-Communist Pope who visits Cuba this week.

This reporter asks whether he has had—like so many other men his age—any troubles with his prostate. "No, no, none at all. I am perfectly healthy," he insists.

So there is no cancer, no heart disease, none of the other health problems of a man in his seventies? "No, no, perfectly healthy," he says again.

In our conversations, he talks about his hopes for Cuba after he is gone. This is a change. Always before, he was unwilling to admit the possibility that he might ever leave power for any reason. Now he makes plans for a successor—his brother Raúl, head of the Cuban military, has been designated—and Fidel Castro even talks a little wistfully about a quiet life free from the demands of his job. He would like to cook again, as he used to do for his friends in college; he would like to read more, to study again, to do a thousand things he's had no time to do since he seized power.

Does this mean he wants to retire? Hastily, he says no. That would not be possible: there is still too much to do.

He doesn't say so, but he seems worried that his revolution will die with him. It is more important to him to show that his regime wasn't merely one dictatorship in the place of another. His regime stood for something, he insists: it stood for justice. He points to education, health care, equality of the races.

But, this reporter replies, Cuban dissidents are jailed, your people can't read the newspapers or books of their choice, their doctors aren't qualified, and, although racial prejudice does seem to have been brought under control, there are still many barriers to any person's freedom and prosperity here.

Castro waves away such concerns. "Without the interference of the United States government," he says, "who knows how much more we will accomplish?"

The future tense. He is still making plans. But he hears the ticking of the clock. And he knows that, for many Americans, his time can't run out soon enough.

SADDAM'S UNCHANGING CHARACTER
November 12, 1997

It's said that only those who don't learn from history are doomed to repeat it, but Iraqi President Saddam Hussein has learned one lesson, and repeated it ever since he invaded Kuwait in 1990: if you cross the line, you may not win much, but chances are excellent that you won't lose much, either.

He plays this game so often, we may have to coin a word: "to saddam," as in, "My saddaming five-year-old reached for the cookies three times after I told him not to."

And so Saddam defies the international law requiring him to dismantle his weapons of mass destruction. Almost nobody believes Saddam has ever complied with that law, and many experts say that Saddam blocks United Nations inspections to buy time: while inspectors wait to enter one site, he moves the contraband somewhere else.

From Saddam's perspective, it's a win-win situation. At best, he'll keep his weapons and drive a wedge between the United States and its allies. At worst, he'll get credit for twitting the U.S. At no time does he believe he'll face punishment worse than the crippling sanctions already in place. And anyway, it's Saddam's people, not Saddam himself, who are really suffering under those sanctions. (If you think he cares about his people's suffering, just recall the way he gassed his Kurdish subjects.)

Saddam's thinking has changed little over the years. This reporter interviewed Saddam in Baghdad shortly after the invasion of Kuwait. At the time, the Iraqi dictator had declared Kuwait a province of Iraq, and expected to hold on to the property permanently.

Confidently, he predicted the United States would never attack him. He was a student of history, he told me, and the Vietnam War had taught him that Americans would never again risk a prolonged, bloody conflict. Western powers might huff and puff, but ultimately he'd be free to add Kuwait's rich oil reserves to his own.

Yes, he was wrong—and yet, when the allies had won the Gulf War, Saddam was allowed to keep power. He never had to face the punishment he feared most, never had to use the private plane that was ready to whisk him off to exile.

There's a tendency, even high in the diplomatic establishment, to personalize the policies of nations, as if Tony Blair could declare war on Jacques Chirac without first seeking the approval of the British Parliament and people. In pluralistic societies, bound by the rule of law, of course that's not the case. But the policies of Iraq really do reflect the thinking of just one man: Saddam himself.

He has built Iraq on a Stalinist model. He doesn't have

much internal support, but his police force is ruthless: who needs support when you can crush dissent?

It was already clear in my interview with him seven years ago that Saddam believes he is the most determined person in the world, and that determination is ultimately what counts. He has benefited repeatedly from the international community's tendency to underestimate his resolve. He has almost never set foot in the West, and yet it doesn't occur to him that he might completely misunderstand the West: he's certain, however, that the West misunderstands him.

He set out to be the dominant power in the Persian Gulf, but then began to imagine himself as a leader for all Islam, on the model of Saladin, who conquered Jerusalem during the Middle Ages. To defeat Israel—and the United States—where others have failed, would crown Saddam's career.

But just to humiliate the United States would make his day. And so he keeps trying, daring the international community to stop him.

THE NEW "GREAT GAME" IN THE CASPIAN SEA
November 5, 1997

If you don't know where the Caspian Sea is, now is a good time to look at the map and familiarize yourself with it. And by all means have the children do the same.

It's there just north of Iran, with shores on Russia's southern border, just east of Turkey and the Black Sea.

Islamic radicalism is on the rise all around it, and so is the new "Great Game."

With little notice—too little—the world's great powers are now maneuvering for position and influence around the Caspian. At stake are fabulously rich oil and gas fields that could completely refocus the world energy picture in the twenty-first century. And because of that, also at stake is future world peace and prosperity.

Until the fall of the old Soviet empire, Russia ruled the region without challenge. But the Kremlin, with its bungling bureaucracy and mind-boggling inefficiency, was never anywhere near able to exploit fully the Caspian's underground riches. And the Communists kept virtually everyone else out.

After the fall, Western capital and know-how came in. First a trickle, now a flood. Lately, China has entered the competition, in a big way, with big bucks.

For the moment, the competition centers around pipelines. Who is going to build them? Where? For whom? Western oil companies know where the oil is. They know what the old Soviets didn't: how to get it out of the ground. What they have yet to figure out is how to get it to market.

China recently agreed to finance a long pipeline to its interior, to help fuel the Chinese drive to become both a world economic and military superpower. The Iranians and Turks want pipelines built through their territories to the Mediterranean and Persian Gulf, for sale of Caspian oil to both Europe and Asia, especially India and Japan.

The Russians and Ukrainians want pipelines through their lands, so they can have access to some of the Caspian oil and send on the rest to Europe, east and west. India, Pakistan, and Afghanistan have their versions of this idea, wanting pipelines for *their* own supplies, and for trans-shipping on to Asia.

The United States, knowing it cannot afford to sit idly by and with its major oil companies already hip-deep in all these power plays, gets more involved by the day.

Charles J. Pittman, chairman and president of Amoco Eurasian Petroleum Company, told this reporter every American should care about these developments because "future rising demands for oil figure to cause upward pressure on prices.

Getting Caspian Sea oil out can dampen those expected price rises—for everybody."

Pittman also points out that developing the economies of newly independent nations in the region, such as Georgia, Azerbaijan, Kazakhstan, and Turkmenistan, promotes stability and peace.

What we have here is something reminiscent of the nineteenth century in two ways. One, the Gold Rush of the mid-1800s (except this is a rush for black gold). Two, the "Great Game."

That's what Rudyard Kipling, in his novel *Kim,* called the contest between Russia and the British for control of the Caspian Sea and Central Asia during most of the 1800s and part of the early twentieth century.

The new "Great Game" that has started in these, the last years of the twentieth century, is destined to continue deep into the early part of the twenty-first.

So much attention is centered right now on the Persian Gulf and troubles with Iraq and Iran, that the rise of the campaigns for control of the Caspian Sea has been nearly ignored.

It won't be for long. Too much is at stake.

THE U.N. AS USUAL: INTRIGUE
AND INFORMATION
October 1, 1997

There is so much going on in the United Nations head-quarters every day that sometimes the boy-reporter in me just wants to run up and down the halls to see what I can find out. Here's an account of one morning when I succumbed to the urge.

Autumn in New York. Wonderful. No wonder they wrote a song about it. The air's growing crisp. Broadway readies new shows. Yankee Stadium rocks.

And along the East River, the United Nations opens its new session. The talky tower of Turtle Bay hums with diplomacy, intrigue—and information.

Others can like or hate the U.N., support or oppose it, but if you're a reporter—if you crave news and chasing stories—you've gotta love it.

Come along with me as a reporter plies his trade in the U.N.'s corridors and council rooms.

It's Tuesday. At the U.N., as at Britain's Parliament, China's Central Committee, and the U.S. Congress, Tuesdays, Wednesdays, and Thursdays are busy. Everything else is just—weekends.

Today the Delegates' Lounge is crowded. Lots of big players, like extras from some James Bond movie, sunk into deep leather chairs. Many of them are smoking, which tells you the Middle East and Asia are especially well represented in the lounge today. Espresso is the house favorite. All coffee at the U.N. is strong enough to float horseshoes. The espresso could soak the hide off a buffalo.

Into a nearby private meeting room with a smashing river view, for a prearranged meeting with the foreign minister of a small Persian Gulf state. He says quietly that France's new oil deal with Iran is "just the beginning of more, bigger trouble France will be causing the U.S. in Iran and Iraq."

The French, he says with a wink, still love women and wine, "but they love independence and money even more."

Time to meet with another veteran diplomat, this one from Asia. "The four-power meeting on the North Korean crisis probably isn't going to happen until sometime next year," he says. "The U.S. hoped to meet this year with both Koreas and China. But it's taken too long to stitch together. And now South Korea's presidential election is too close."

Another source confirms this story, then adds that the bigger news making the rounds of cloakrooms today is that "the Chinese will soon announce they are releasing two of the best-known dissidents they've imprisoned.

"This is to give Clinton some help before his big meeting with [Chinese President] Jiang Zemin this fall. It's a little sweetener, in hopes of softening up American public opinion and Congress."

A check with other sources indicates this story is probably true (and it may even be announced by the time you read this column).

Next, the foreign minister of a Latin American country. On "background," he reveals the U.S. ambassador to the U.N. will be meeting later in the day with the Cuban foreign minister, Roberto Robaina. First time any such high-level diplomats from these two countries have met officially in years.

But it turns out, there may be less to this than indicated. Bill Richardson, America's main man at the U.N., had to honor Cuba's request for a meeting. He was president of the Security Council for the month. He had no choice.

When that meeting is over, the official word from both sides is that terrorism against Havana hotels was discussed. But might this meeting lead to something bigger between the Clinton administration and Cuba?

Later, back in the Delegates' Lounge and down in the cafeteria, well-placed sources from several other countries opine that, yes, President Clinton might consider adjusting policies toward Cuba, at least a little.

But, they cautioned, "it's unlikely. And if it's even going to be considered seriously, that won't happen until after the Pope's trip to Cuba in January."

Ahh, New York in autumn. Broadway and baseball at their best. And, if you love the hunt for news, it's prime time at the U.N., too.

The Chinese waited several more weeks before releasing any notable dissidents—namely until shortly before

President Clinton's trip to Beijing in June 1998. I interviewed one, Wang Dan, for a column reprinted on page 79.

INDEPENDENCE WON,
OPPORTUNITIES LOST
August 13, 1997

Only a few months after I wrote this column, India and Pakistan's history took a new and disturbing turn: toward a nuclear arms race. As these recollections may serve to underscore, the hostility between these two countries is of long duration and deep—and makes their current rivalry all the more dangerous.

This was as evident as ever in August 1999, when long-standing border skirmishing in the disputed province of Kashmir heated up, culminating in the downing of a Pakistani military plane by an Indian fighter jet. And when the United States and some other concerned nations brokered a truce, Pakistan's armed forces viewed their forced withdrawal from the province as a betrayal by their government . . . a factor in driving a military coup just months later.

This week (August 14–15), India and Pakistan mark the fiftieth anniversary of their independence from Britain—and from each other.

Under British imperial rule, the two countries had been one. But in a wrenching series of negotiations, they split over a difference in religion. Pakistan was to be primarily a Muslim state; India was to be primarily Hindu.

Negotiations and nationhood didn't end the disputes between the two peoples. There have been three wars between India and Pakistan, the most recent in 1971.

This reporter doesn't pretend to be an expert on these two countries. However, I covered the second India-Pakistan war in 1965. And what I saw told me a lot about the realities, and the potentials, of these two countries.

We had to drive out to the battlefront, outside a city that has been a flashpoint of conflict between the two countries: on the Pakistani side, the city is called Lahore. On the Indian side of the border, the city is Amritsar. The battle was east of Amritsar.

I'd seen a skirmish, but never a war. Suddenly here was one bursting all around me. It was like watching a deadly movie. Planes were dogfighting overhead, and tanks dueling in the sand just up the road.

It was plain to see the Indians had the older equipment, but they could maneuver better, darting like a mongoose. The Pakistanis had more firepower, able to strike like the cobra. If the cobra could just keep the mongoose pinned down, the Pakistanis would win.

It was not to be. In a single day, I counted more than forty destroyed Pakistani tanks. Leadership and mobility made the difference. The Indian officers had better training, used their equipment more efficiently, and moreover had the advantage of fighting on their own turf. Within a few weeks, the Indian counteroffensive had pushed back the Pakistani incursions there in the northwest.

That first battle taught me a lesson that would be proven again in other battles I would see, from Vietnam to Afghanistan to Kuwait to Bosnia: mobility and motivation can often beat heavier firepower.

But some of the other lessons I learned in those days had little to do with war.

I had never seen such poverty and sickness as I saw in India in 1965. The degree of human misery is almost impossible to describe. So many people were starving, sick, desperately poor—or all of the above.

I was also impressed by the hatred between Indians and Pakistanis. I remember marveling that the two countries weren't at war all the time, every day.

What potential lay in these countries' hands! If the people could be employed and fed, if the people could work together, Hindus and Muslims side by side instead of at each other's throats, then it seemed there was nothing they might not accomplish.

The potential is still there—and too little developed.

Too often, Americans tend to ignore what goes on in India and Pakistan, until there's a famine or disaster of some kind. But we do so at our peril.

This is not only because India and Pakistan are so populous, with nuclear options and the power to wage devastating war.

Both countries deserve our attention and our respect because we have much in common. Like the United States, these were large colonies who broke away from British rule. Both countries offer myriad potential resources—and markets for American goods.

And, perhaps most important, many families who are American today—came from India or Pakistan only yesterday.

They will be celebrating the independence, and the peace, between India and Pakistan. So should the rest of us.

WAITING FOR LIGHT
May 5, 1999

BELGRADE, YUGOSLAVIA—It was a clear, moonlit night over the May Day holiday weekend in this capital. Serbs stayed up late in the spring warmth, drinking espresso at outdoor cafes, partying, visiting each other's homes.

Then the lights went out. Everywhere. Nobody panicked. But everybody worried, and a lot of people who had not really been afraid before during this war, suddenly got afraid.

The night the lights went out—late Sunday, May 2, into early Monday, May 3—is as close as we've come to a turning point in this war. For the first time, American bombers knocked out electricity in Belgrade and in most of Serbia. They used a so-called soft bomb filled with carbon filaments, a hitherto secret weapon, that short-circuited Serbia's main power grid without destroying it.

Serbs didn't know immediately what hit them. At first they believed, because they wanted to believe, that this might be some run-of-the-mill power outage. They quickly found out that it was the work of bombing runs, although they didn't know what kind.

Anger and outrage mixed with deepening concern and fear as the night wore on. Electricity and regular water supplies stayed off, and telephone service was interrupted.

"I'm really scared for the first time," a young woman in her twenties told me as we and a group of others scanned the sky. "It's getting worse, this bombing. Is it ever going to stop?"

She is not an admirer of Serbian leader Slobodan Milosevic. Never has been. But, as is overwhelmingly the case with most Serbs, she has rallied behind his defiance of NATO. It is a matter of patriotic pride.

But she's shaken now and makes no attempt to hide it.

That's the mood of Belgrade now. The Serbs are in no mood for surrender. But they are more concerned than they were, and the fear factor is rising.

A young man in the group—he's thirty-five—cursed expertly in English. "What are the people supposed to do? Our country is really poor, you know. Now we are being made poorer. The whole infrastructure of our country is being systematically destroyed. Not just our bridges and rail lines, but everything. Tonight, the power plants. Tomorrow, who knows?"

(He didn't, couldn't yet know that the new weapon dropped this night had not in fact destroyed the country's main power facility.)

The young man cursed more and took another shot of Yugoslavian plum brandy. He wasn't drunk and didn't intend to become so. But he continued to curse.

He glared hard at this American reporter and said between clenched teeth, "I hope you and your countrymen know that we take this very personally. We will not forget it."

This young man, and every other of the many Serbs with whom your reporter spoke, categorically rejected the argument that the air campaign is directed at the Milosevic dictatorship and its policies of ethnic cleansing—and not at the Serbian people.

The Serbs dispute what the rest of the world has seen. They refuse to believe that the systematic "ethnic cleansing" in Kosovo has actually happened, and continues to happen.

They are in denial: massive, national denial. As incredible as it seems to most outsiders, the Serbs see themselves and their fellow countrymen as victims in Kosovo, not perpetrators.

Ask them about documented atrocities, and the Serbs will tell you it's propaganda, faked—or else they'll change the subject and tell you the Kosovar Albanians are guilty of much worse crimes.

And so they drink and deny, and curse and scan the sky, and wait for light in Belgrade.

STRANGERS ON A TRAIN
July 2, 1997

HONG KONG, CHINA—You meet the nicest people on trains. This has been my experience since childhood days in

Texas, riding on the likes of the *Sam Houston Zephyr* and the *Sunset Limited*.

Trouble is, in the United States these days there are so few good trains, and the pace of life is so hurried and harried, that you don't have much chance of meeting nice people on trains.

This came to mind the other day as I was riding through the Chinese countryside on the new Beijing-to-Hong Kong express. Unofficially known as the *Hong Kong Cannonball*. It's the newest train in China, built to speed along a whole new rail line. The route was specifically laid out to slice through parts of the eastern China countryside far inland from the economically booming seacoast.

The idea is to have this new rail link do for the interior of China what railroads did for the interior of the United States in the late 1800s. Namely, open the country to development, nurture it to grow and thrive.

New railroad towns spring up along the route. Old towns take on new energy and hope. Products and people move faster, easier. Growth along the coast begins penetrating into the nation's interior. This was America's experience. China hopes it will be their experience, too, with this new line.

I left Beijing right on time at 9:30 P.M., with reservations in the best sleeper section. The accommodations weren't lavish, unless you compared them with everybody else's on the train. In third class, people either sleep sitting up—or else they don't sleep.

Despite the comparative comforts of my bunk, sleep would not come, and I found myself wandering the train, looking for people with whom to talk.

One man was willing, but it turns out he didn't speak English. I don't speak Chinese. That didn't matter much to him: he talked anyway.

One woman was eager, but she was a cardsharp, so that didn't work out, either.

Then I met Yang Guo Fung. He trades stocks on the Shenzhen exchange. Shenzhen is another of China's booming coastal cities, not far from Hong Kong. Yang Guo Fung's specialties are stocks of companies headquartered in southern China. He's been up north, hustling new clients in Beijing, and is now on the long ride back home.

It turns out Yang Guo Fung is one of China's new rich. He's made a small fortune in Chinese stocks, and is driving to make it larger.

"Annual return of just over fifty percent last year," he says through our interpreter. "Technology and real estate–based equities are performing best." And he goes on to say he thinks he'll do even better in the year ahead.

He's in his early forties, dressed in an expensive but unpretentious suit. And his story checked out.

Coastal Chinese cities are beginning to have increasing numbers of young people like him: Chinese yuppies. If China's vast, poverty-ravaged, and underdeveloped interior is to be developed, Yang Guo Fung and those in the new generation like him are key. They have the vision, they have the drive, and the know-how to get the investment money China so desperately needs.

"Not quite so desperately now," says Yang Guo Fung. "Hong Kong coming back into China will be an enormous help. Many in the West may not realize how much financial muscle Hong Kong adds to us.

"The China boom," he says, "is about to take off all over again." He smiled, handed me his business card, and went back to his laptop.

Out the window of the *Hong Kong Cannonball,* China slept. But for how much longer?

A VISIT TO THE GOOD EARTH
June 25, 1997

HUANG GONG, CHINA—Deep in the interior of southeast China, far from the booming coastal areas you read and hear so much about, light years from the glitter of Hong Kong, nobody is rich. Everybody is poor.

This is farm country—"Good Earth" country, after the novel by Pearl Buck. People have been living and working this land in much the same way, using much the same tools, for thousands of years. The hoes and rakes they use are museum pieces.

It is a land where the buffalo roam—water buffalo. These beasts of burden have done heavy farm work in this region for as far back as history records.

In the twenty-four hours spent in the area, this reporter saw not a single tractor. Plowing and other field preparation is by buffalo or oxen. Planting and harvesting is by hand. And backs. Human backs. Men, women, and children, all day every day, work the fields. If, as a family, they make $200 a year— they are above average. If, a few told me, any family makes $400 a year, they are at or near the top.

Much, perhaps too much, is written these days about change in China. A lot has changed in the country, especially in major cities along and near the coast. Here, in the interior, things are different. Bleaker. Less promising. There is little food, less money. The poverty has never changed.

"My ancestors worked this land, just as I am working it," a farmer named Chu says. "But the land was richer then. It takes more to get the land to produce less now."

He speaks of hopes for his children. He has two. "They must get schooling," he says, "lots of schooling." But the local schools are poor. It costs more now, the farmers have to pay extra tuition, and the price recently went up again, says farmer Chu.

"If this is capitalism," he says through an interpreter, "then I don't like it." He says that yes, he has heard of boom-times in cities along the coast. But he adds he doesn't know whether to believe it or not.

Then he goes back to tilling the field. Not a dry field—you don't plant rice in dry ground—but knee-deep in water the color of chocolate milk. The water buffalo goes first. He is yoked to a wooden contraption that paddles through the mud, and the farmer rides atop like a charioteer, steering with a string he's attached to the buffalo's nose.

Once the field has been prepared, the women come. Squat, hard women, they plant rice shoots by hand so fast their arms are a blur. Hour after hour. Their backs nearly folded in half. One of them agrees to answer a few questions as she works.

"What is the greatest need in this village?"

"Schools. Better schools. Our children have no chance unless our schools get better, much better, quickly.

"And water. This is not our worst year, but water is a problem. If we had more water, we could plant and harvest twice a year. We only have enough water for doing it once. There must be a way to get more water."

She never takes her eyes off her work. Her hands never slow.

I ask the farmers about the future—about their Communist government's plans for spreading economic boom-times, and the return of Hong Kong to China's control. These are headlines in newspapers around the world, although only two of the dozens of farmers I talk to could read even one word. Will any of it make a difference in their lives?

Sure, they say, they've heard the government's promises of prosperity. But so far, they've seen no real change. The supposedly booming, changing Chinese economy hasn't touched Huang Gong.

Life and work in the Good Earth go on as they have—for centuries.

ECONOMIC FORECAST FOR JAPAN— FROM A SURPRISING SOURCE
June 17, 1998

"Japan's ability to stabilize its economy and begin slogging back is the absolute key to any comeback by the Asian economy as a whole," says Li Lu. "And also essential to the continued health of the U.S. economy."

Li Lu is Chinese, one of the leaders of the movement for freedom and democracy that climaxed in Tiananmen Square in 1989.

He was a student in China then, one of China's best, brightest, and bravest. After China's dictatorship crushed the freedom movement with tanks, he escaped to the U.S.

He learned English, raced through Columbia University's undergraduate, business, and law schools, and now, nine years later, is a millionaire entrepreneur running a Wall Street hedge fund.

His is an amazing story, a great American success story with a Chinese accent. His appreciation for America and its people is deep. With it, he will return to China someday, a leader of its new Tiananmen generation.

But this day, he is talking with your reporter about Japan as well as China. China's economic future is closely intertwined with that of Japan, he points out. But not as closely intertwined as those of Japan and the United States.

Japan is the world's second most powerful economic superpower. It is not too much to say, as many in Washington and on Wall Street do, that as Japan's economy goes, eventually so goes our own.

And Japan's economy is now, officially, in recession. If the Japanese recession cuts much deeper and lasts much longer, and most especially if it sinks into outright depression (as much of Asia already has), then the U.S. economy will be significantly affected.

This is not a prediction of doom, says Li Lu. It is a yellow flag of caution about a building danger.

"The time is near when the United States must step in with a massive infusion of financial aid to Japan. When the moment comes, Americans should not be surprised," Li Lu said. "And they should understand that it's in their own interest."

He couldn't know how soon his predictions would start coming true. Fewer than twenty-four hours after he said that, Treasury Secretary Bob Rubin announced the spending of U.S. dollars to support the yen. And headlines now shout that more such action may be necessary.

"In this, timing is everything," Li Lu says. "If the move's too soon, the money will be wasted. But wait too long, and it will also be wasted."

President Clinton and Secretary Rubin decided this was the time. They've rolled the dice. So now, while Clinton is touring China, he'll be sweating out the news from Japan.

Li Lu believes the timing of President Clinton's trip to China this month is wrong. It gives China's Communist leaders too much for too little in return, and threatens to slow what Li Lu sees as China's inevitable march toward truly representative government.

American business leaders, he thinks, are wrong not to support more pressure on China's leaders for more human rights and political reform, faster.

He worries about that, but for the moment he is at least as worried about Japan's economy as he is about what is happening inside China.

Over the long pull of history, China's importance to world peace and prosperity, and thus to the future of our own country, is immense.

But so is Japan's. And in the short-to-medium pull of history, what happens to Japan—especially to Japan's economy— is more important than what happens to China.

Li Lu, student hero turned millionaire and future Chinese leader, is watching closely. The rest of us should be, too.

THE CHINA CONNECTION—TO IRAN
June 11, 1997

Several months after his election, Iranian President Mohammed Khatami began making tentative movements toward improved relations with the United States. There remain profound differences between the two countries, but Khatami's gestures were the first and most positive yet in the two decades of hostility. As of this writing, the Clinton administration was still moving cautiously, afraid that Khatami's overtures might be empty, a trick, or might close down again under pressure from Iran's conservative mullahs. Even if the overture is sincere, State Department officials and others have asked, how can the U.S. appear to condone a state that continues to sponsor terrorism and to oppose our political, economic, and diplomatic interests worldwide?

At the time the following column was written, Khatami had just been elected, and had not yet made any attempt to improve Iran's relations with the United States.

Everybody is talking about China and Hong Kong these days. Well, not everybody. His Highness Sheikh Hamad bin Khalifa Al-Thani, the emir of Qatar, is sitting in his hotel suite, talking with a reporter about China and *Iran.*

"China is a major supplier of weapons to Iran, including missiles," he says. He worries about China's growing influence with Iran. In his part of the world, many leaders worry about the consequences of any Chinese-Iranian alliance, which is believed to be key not only to Iran's designs to spread Islamic fundamentalism throughout the Middle East, but also to China's drive to supplant the United States and Japan as the dominant military and economic power of the Pacific.

But there may have been some important changes since Iran's presidential election in May. The surprise winner was Mohammed Khatami, a fifty-four-year-old mullah. He is widely described as a moderate. Which doesn't mean he is friendly to the U.S.—only that he defeated the more radical candidate favored by hard-line followers of the late Ayatollah Khomeini. President Khatami drew impressive support from young people, intellectuals, and others eager for relief from repressive religious rule.

All of which has stirred a new debate about what the U.S. should do: ease economic sanctions? try for diplomatic dialogue with Iran? or maintain the present policy of trying to isolate and punish Iran as a terrorist state?

Qatar's emir takes a deep breath before commenting. He is forty-seven years old, and has been emir for barely two years. He was educated partly in England, which is where he got the hand-tailored suit he wears this day instead of his traditional robes and headdress. This is his first visit to North America.

His country is tiny—a city-state, really. Qatar borders Saudi Arabia to the south, and extends northward along a highly strategic position along the west coast of the Persian Gulf: its proximity to the Strait of Hormuz provides access to the Gulf of Oman and the Arabian Sea.

Through this strait, gulf, and sea flows much of the oil upon which Japan and the West, including the United States, depend.

Since America's defeat of Iraq, Iran has been beefing up forces and installing better weapons around the strait and elsewhere in the region. China has helped.

"With all of this going on, and especially in light of Iran's recent election, perhaps it is time to reflect and respond in some new ways," says the emir.

He measures his words carefully, in good but inexpert English. He emphasizes he is not telling the U.S. what to do. "It is only my opinion, but a sign of new flexibility by America just now might pay big dividends." He believes that such a sign could strengthen the base that elected Khatami, and drain internal support for Iran's most radical elements.

What kind of sign? Well, he goes on to say, "almost anything that would signal that the people of the United States are not hostile to the people of Iran, that Americans seek to be friends, not foes, of the Iranian people." Just offering to talk at some meaningful diplomatic level would be a useful start, he thinks.

"A first move by America with something such as this might make an enormous difference for their new leader."

He has communicated these opinions privately to President Clinton. In the meantime, the debate builds in this country over what to do about Iran. Is this the right moment for change? Will there ever be a right moment?

And to complicate matters, as the emir and others point out, there is a Chinese connection.

THE NEW MISÉRABLES
May 20, 1998

Exactly thirty years after student and worker uprisings brought France to a standstill and threatened to rewrite the history of Europe, I returned to Paris. Nobody wanted to talk about 1968—they were too concerned with the present.

PARIS—Springtime in the City of Lights is different this year. For one thing, it is hot. Unusually hot, unusually often, unusually early in the year.

Along the boulevards and in the bistros, El Niño gets its share of blame. So does global warming. The French being the French, they blame Americans—our cars and our industries—for much of that.

France's love-hate relationship with America and things American is alive and well. Down deep, the French are everlastingly grateful for what America did twice this century to save France from the Germans, and they admire us.

"What you did to move yourselves to the forefront of the Technological Age was amazing," a government official told your reporter. "And now, as we move deep into the Information Era, you have done it once again—moved to the front and kept yourselves there.

"France has a lot of technological know-how, more than most Americans realize," he went on. "And we also moved quickly and pretty well in the early stages of the information revolution—with our telephone system, for example.

"But somehow, we never seem able to leverage our advantages. We never seem able to break through and surge ahead in world markets. Part of it may be a lack of the kind of huge capital America can always muster. Another part may be that we are, after all, a small country with a small domestic market base. Because of that, we're seldom able to build a springboard into worldwide competition."

But he admits there is much more to it than that. So do other French men and women with whom a reporter talks, people in academia, journalism, and science. Some of the problem, they all agree, is a matter of drive.

France has a good education system, but they think it's dangerously old-fashioned at the university and postgraduate levels. And they believe the system falls short in instilling a determined work ethic.

"It isn't that we lack discipline as a nation," one university student told me. "We lack drive, determination, and national will. And we are woefully short on leadership. France's leadership doesn't connect with the rest of the industrialized world."

With this student and others, the word "ennui" was used liberally to describe what they think is the national mood and a large part of what's wrong. It's a French word meaning "boredom," and the listlessness and dissatisfaction that result from boredom.

"There is ennui and also fear, fear of being left out and left behind," one newspaperman said. "Increasingly, many of the best of our young people no longer believe they can become rich or famous by remaining in France. They love France, but they see it as a museum or retirement home. So they either quit trying to achieve, drop out, or they flee."

A lawyer lamented, "Great Britain had its Margaret Thatcher to yank it into competitiveness and instill a new national pride and will. We are hobbled by an outdated, mostly socialist system of regulation and entitlement. We have yet to have our Thatcher. And there's none in sight."

His friend, also a lawyer, added, "You Americans have had boosts from both Ronald Reagan and Bill Clinton. One old man and one young one. We haven't had anything close to either. We're still looking, still searching, still hoping for a French revival and renewal. But the world is passing us by."

Your reporter leaves convinced that the French are creating their own Lost Generation: slackers or exiles, they can't see any means to succeed at home. They're the new Misérables: needy, numerous—and ready for change.

Chapter 3

THE WASHINGTON
SCENE: POLITICS
AND POLITICIANS

From January 1998 to February 1999, much of my reporting time was given over to one of the strangest stories I've ever encountered: the collision of Republican Special Prosecutor Ken Starr's grand jury investigation with President Clinton's private life. Some called it "Lewinskygate," others called it disgusting. The story broke on January 21, 1998, when allegations first appeared about the President's affair with former White House intern Monica Lewinsky, and moved so quickly at first that one couldn't be sure if facts reported one day would be valid even a few hours later. After more than a year of near-paralysis in Washington, the issue was finally put to rest when the Senate voted to acquit in the President's impeachment trial.

But the scandal's aftermath lingers on in American politics and may heat up again in the thick of the 2000 general election campaign. It will doubtless attach itself permanently to President Clinton's name in histories of our time. Congress, too, has had its eye blackened by the role it played in what was widely viewed as an overly politicized impeachment process. No one seemed blameless in this tawdry spectacle and everyone, including the American public and the media, lost in the end.

As of this writing, Kenneth Starr has just stepped down from the special prosecutor post as what started out as the Whitewater probe marches on without him. He has left it to his successor, Robert Ray, to issue the investigation's final report, due out who-knows-when. In the original edition of Deadlines and Datelines, I wrote that the speed of this story made me uncertain which pieces to include. Now that the drama has run its immediate course, I face the same problem, as well as that of trying to weigh how much prominence to give it here. Though it was surely one of the biggest stories of recent years, history provides little guidance as to how its importance—and the actions of its players—will ultimately be judged. Despite the modern mania to attach the suffix "-gate" to every scandal, the parallels between President Clinton's transgressions and Nixon's are relatively few (though both made their situations worse by trying to cover up their actions).

The behavior of most journalists on this story also bore sadly little resemblance to that of those covering Watergate. The press as a whole won few admirers for their work here. We depended on rumor and innuendo, reported as fact information that was suspect or inadequately confirmed, and (in far too many cases) wallowed in the lurid atmosphere. We might have risen to our responsibilities, acted as models of decorum, helped our fellow citizens during a time of confusion and crisis—but we seldom did.

I have included the following three essays as examples of how one working reporter tried to cover a story that was troubling both in itself and in its implications for our country.

LIVES OF THE HUNTED
September 16, 1998

Ernest Thompson Seton once wrote a book called *Lives of the Hunted*.

The Clintons are now living it.

Ken Starr has hit President Clinton with his best shot. He has badly wounded him and has him staggering. But the President is still standing. Limping, wobbling, and near collapse, but still standing.

Now Starr is pressing, trying to put the political kill-shot on him. Starr has many more shots to fire. They include unloading on First Lady Hillary Clinton.

Tucked away in Starr's voluminous report to Congress is the warning, the threat, and the reminder that he is continuing to investigate other phases of what he considers to be possible criminal acts by both Clintons.

Starr reported: "Evidence is being gathered on . . . the Rose Law Firm's representation of Madison Guaranty Savings and Loan Association. . . . All phases of the investigation are now nearing completion."

This refers directly to, in Starr's words, "legal work done by the Rose Law Firm, including the First Lady" (a partner in the firm) on the Arkansas "Whitewater" real estate deal in the 1980s.

The public may long ago have tired of the whole Whitewater business, but Starr hasn't. He reportedly has believed for a long time that he has enough evidence to indict Mrs. Clinton in that complex case.

Unlike the President's situation, where the law is unclear about whether, and if so when, a President can be indicted, there's no legal reason Hillary Clinton can't be indicted while her husband is still in office.

Politically, it could be risky for Starr to do such a thing. But the possibility of his doing so worries the Clintons plenty. The threat is a major factor in their thinking now. It has to be. It is one of the generally unrecognized pressures on the President to resign.

While Congress ponders what to do, Starr just keeps coming. He is relentless. And, as the Clintons see it, merciless and pitiless in his partisan political zeal. Nothing short of driving them from office and destroying them both politically will satisfy him and those who back him—that's the view both Clintons have expressed privately to friends.

Starr naturally sees his role differently. He views truth and justice as his mission. The law, not politics, is his duty as he has described it. And about pursuing truth and justice, he has no apology, as he tells all who will listen.

For Starr, these are days of victory and vindication. The old Southern phrase "smiling like a deacon with four aces" comes to mind. The Clintons took him on, head-on, and he beat them.

But his defeat of them is not yet complete. So he aims now for the kill-shot. Some Republicans and many Democrats don't want him to take it. But the choice isn't theirs. Congress doesn't control Starr. No one does. That's the meaning of "independent counsel." The law says so.

When the smoke from all of this finally clears, that law may be changed. Politicians in both parties tell this reporter they now shudder to think where the independent counsel law could lead in future investigations. But that's of little if any real help to the Clintons.

They've been hit. Crippling shot. And their pursuer still has them in his crosshairs. They are the hunted, and the hunter is closing in, looking for the one, final shot that will put them away. *Forever.*

If the Clintons make it out of this bloody political corner they are now in (and into which, in many ways, they put themselves), it will be a survival story worthy of Ernest Thompson Seton.

TWO AGAINST THE WORLD
July 29, 1998

WASHINGTON, D.C.—Inside the White House, it's two against the world. Bill and Hillary, the President and the First Lady. More than ever, now that Monica Lewinsky and her mother have agreed to help Ken Starr.

When the news reached the White House that Lewinsky would receive immunity from prosecution in return for her testimony before Starr's grand jury, the President's staff was thrown into gloom. Two longtime Clinton confidants told this reporter that day: "There have been dark times around here before, but this is the darkest." And both said the Clintons never before have felt so alone. But both confidants emphasized that, as one put it, "[The Clintons] are determined to tough it out, fight to the finish, and prevail." "Prevail" means finish their term in office.

The Clintons have long been convinced Starr is out to get them. He failed in every effort. Then, near the start of this year, came the break about some kind of relationship between Lewinsky and the President. That breathed new life into Starr's investigations. But as long as Lewinsky wasn't talking, Starr was stymied.

Now she is talking. A lot. As a result, the Clinton presidency has been moved into a new and more perilous position. The Clintons know it. Their whole history as a married couple has been forged in the fires of political heat. But they have never been through heat this hot.

They now must make a long march through a scorching valley in the shadow of political death.

Washington is once again filled with whispers of the possibility—the real possibility—of impeachment or resignation. Some of those whispers come from the White House itself.

Among the staff, doubt and fear are spreading like mildew in a damp basement. In this atmosphere, the Clintons know that ultimately they can depend only upon themselves. It's the two of them against the world.

Among those who know best, it is said that this is the way they view the situation: they must fight on three fronts—legal, political, and historical.

Legally, they expect Starr to try for an actual indictment of the President. They believe Starr would also indict the First Lady if he thought he could. But against her, he doesn't have enough. So goes the belief. But against Mr. Clinton, Starr—now that he has Lewinsky talking—has enough to tempt him to go for indictment.

Politically, the Clintons are said to be convinced that Starr will submit a voluminous case to the Republican-controlled House of Representatives and will argue that it lays out a "constitutional crisis" worthy of impeachment consideration. No one in the White House, least of all the Clintons, underestimates the ominous potential this has. Everybody in the White House, most of all the Clintons, is furious about this, believing it to be grossly unfair, but they recognize the real and present danger it represents.

If the Democrats should win back control of the House in November's midterm elections, that could change dramatically the equation in the Clintons' favor. But they can't count on it. The odds against its happening are too long.

On the historical front, the Clintons are said to be absolutely convinced that history will view Starr's case as a political vendetta, built on shaky evidence of minor wrongdoings at most, and bankrolled by wealthy ideologues who hate all the Clintons have tried to accomplish.

Hope, clearly, is the father of this expectation. As the siege tightens and the climatic, decisive battles draw nearer, the Clintons cling to that hope.

Together. Angry. In the last decisive fight to hold together what's left of their dreams, two against the world.

LISTENING TO AMERICA, ONE-ON-ONE
February 3, 1999

Americans generally are up and optimistic these days. Why wouldn't they be?

Unemployment is low. Inflation is practically nonexistent. Interest rates are low. The stock markets are up. And while many troubles around the world pose dangers to U.S. national security, the Cold War is long gone and there is no one overwhelming international military threat.

Your reporter has been traveling the country these past weeks, coast to coast and border to border. Seldom if ever has he found so many Americans in so many different walks of life feeling so good about themselves and the country.

But that doesn't mean they are blasé, smug, or self-satisfied. They are mad as hell about what is happening in Washington, for one thing. Time after time, in personal interviews and conversations, Americans in a wide range of situations said they were sick of hearing what the President has done *and* the Republican drive to remove him from office.

"It's a mudslide, an avalanche of muck," said a waitress in Los Angeles. "The House, the Senate, the President, and his people—the whole lot of them—should be ashamed of themselves. And we should be ashamed of them."

An electrician in Detroit said, "President Clinton has disgraced himself, his family, his office, and our country. That gang of Republicans after him is just as bad, maybe worse. I can't stand any of them, on either side."

"They're mad, just plumb crazy, the whole lot of them in Washington," a Houston-area cattleman told me in Texas.

A small businessman in Arkansas said, "I'm so sick of the Clintons—Bill, Hillary, and all their helpers and hangers-on—I could scream. But the Republicans are so hypocritical and mean, they almost make the Clintons and their crowd look good."

In Georgia, a farmer said, "That Ken Starr is nothing but a prissy prude of a hit man. He and the Republicans who put him in there are about nothing but hate, revenge, and getting even for elections they lost.

"I don't like Clinton, never have. Can't stand him. But this man Starr, and that Henry Hyde—that whole bunch makes my stomach turn.

"What's happened to our country? These people are all terrible."

And so it went with most people in most places in more than four weeks of travel.

Yes, some spoke glowingly of the President. And some others supported the Republicans, including Ken Starr. But they were a distinct minority.

This was not a poll. Just a reporter moving around, talking to people where they worked.

These Americans do have worries besides Washington.

Schools, for one thing. There's a general feeling that American schools need drastic improvement in a hurry.

"Our kids aren't being prepared for the international competition of the twenty-first century," an insurance-selling grandmother in New Jersey said.

Drugs are another overriding worry. "We kept spending money and passing drug laws," said a Chicago stockbroker, "but the problem keeps getting worse."

A longtime convict in one major state prison said, "Mr. Rather, let me tell you, drugs are all over our prisons."

How do people in prison get drugs? she was asked. "You figure it out," she answered with a stare.

And people naturally worry how long the good economic times can last, how much it will hurt when the economy slows or plunges downward.

When you travel the country and listen to America, the mood is good. But the people have no illusions about the existence of some very real problems. And they do have fears. The biggest one being that Washington has turned so wacky and nasty that no one there is listening.

THINKING ABOUT THINKING ABOUT IT
February 24, 1999

It's something every reporter knows: politics don't keep. The shelf life of political pieces is woefully short and, in comparison, book lead times are deadly long.

Still, I don't feel I can ignore Campaign 2000 altogether . . . especially since it started a good three years in advance, making it a long-running story indeed. When this edition comes out, the races will be coming toward the finish line at the respective summer nominating conventions . . . which may just be a foregone conclusion by that time.

I'd probably be smartest just to leave the election alone here, lest I have to eat more than my daily allowance of words and predictions gone sour. But somehow I can't just leave well enough alone. The McCain piece in itself—dated even as I write this (Fred Thompson? Colin Powell?)—serves, in its way, as a perfect example of the speed at which electoral politics move now. Yet its focus on campaign finance reform makes it, sadly, as timely as ever.

I could not have known when I wrote this piece how right I was in saying that "the important decisions about money and support are being made right now." I take no joy in noting this, as the process as it stands now raises serious questions about the health of our democracy. And in the absence of any fund-raising reforms—McCain's or anyone else's—passing Congress, the situation isn't going to change anytime soon.

So, with the election being called even now (fall 1999), months before a single primary vote has even been cast, I throw caution to the wind in order to at least give a taste of this highly unusual—and troubling—election season. I start with a bit of gallows humor.

This is to informally announce that I am considering a bid for the presidency.

In my formal announcement, to be made in Cowsbottom, Texas, and again later the same day on *Larry King Live,* I will say the same thing without splitting the infinitive "to announce."

But since this is only an informal announcement, I can split any infinitive I want. I may even end a sentence with a preposition, if I can remember what one is.

Later this month I will announce that I am meeting with my advisers to decide whether to announce that I am forming a committee, to explore whether to announce that I am setting up a campaign organization, prior to announcing that I am running for the highest office in the land.

The meeting, the committee, and the organization will all be staffed by more or less the same advisers (code names: Larry, Curly, and Moe). But by delaying the announcement of the formation of the organization, I won't have to pay them.

Thus, you should not take this informal announcement as an announcement that I'm actually running. No, no, no. You should take this informal announcement as an announcement that I'm thinking about thinking about it.

This follows my announcements, both formal and informal, at two-week intervals for the past two years, to the effect that I was thinking about thinking about thinking about it.

These announcements are my little way to get my name in the papers, radio, and television as often as possible without buying an ad.

My only fear is that Larry King will get sick of me before I can formally announce that I'm exploring thinking about announcing.

As I look out across the happy faces of the good people of

the great state of (choose one: Iowa, New Hampshire), I have already made up my mind to launch my campaign. But I'm not going to come out and say so.

That would be telling.

Therefore, informally, over the next few weeks, following the swimsuit and evening wear competitions, I will *not* announce that I have filed all necessary campaign papers, as well as financial records and sexual history, with the Federal Election Commission.

As a possibly potential candidate, I've spent an average of 182.5 days per year here in the great state of (choose one: Iowa, New Hampshire) since 1996.

Sheer coincidence!

So far, the single greatest obstacle to my candidacy is my beloved wife, who has no desire to see me in public office.

The second greatest obstacle to my candidacy is the American people, who also have no desire to see me in public office.

I've known flu germs who stood a better chance of being elected to the White House.

However, as recent events in Washington demonstrate, politics no longer have anything to do with what the public wants.

So unfurl the bunting! Who cares whether I've got my bunting license yet?

Campaign costs in the year 2000 are expected to exceed $1 billion—more cash than I have on me just now. So you may wonder, "How will Dan *pay* for this potential bid?"

My response is, "I won't—*you* will." Armed representatives of my campaign staff will be going door-to-door for your contributions.

Some may protest, saying this violates campaign finance rules.

And my response is, "*What* rules?" You didn't really *believe* all that stuff about regulation and reform, did you? Those guys in the Senate are such kidders.

In conclusion, I want to highlight an important difference between my possibly declarable, potential candidacy and all the others you read about:

I'm joking.

UNDERESTIMATED FEATURES
July 30, 1997

The Vice President is on the telephone, wanting to talk about the new budget.

Al Gore is probably aware that, to many people, root canal surgery would sound like more fun than such a conversation.

But the budget is serious business—if it were fun, there'd be something wrong with it—and the Vice President lured me to the phone with promises of illuminating several "underestimated features" of the new agreement.

He sounded relaxed, and I could hear him smiling. The new budget deal had just been settled. If Al Gore had any concerns about campaign finance hearings, check-waving Buddhist nuns, or the legion of *other* Washingtonians eager to take credit for the country's first balanced budget deal in a generation—you wouldn't have known it.

Make no mistake: Al Gore is *excited* about this budget agreement.

The budget, he said, will "restore fairness to the way our country treats legal immigrants." He stressed the word "legal," putting vocal italics on the whole phrase "legal immigrants."

"Medicaid and other disability and health benefits were being wiped out for legal immigrants who are currently receiving assistance or had become disabled," he said. "This budget restores [the aid]. Most Americans did not want legal immigrants who are hurting, to fear being turned out of their apartments or nursing homes, or otherwise made to suffer.

"But most Americans were not aware this was in the process of happening. It was an underreported story, not widely known. However, especially among American families of Hispanic and Asian heritage, it was a big worry and a huge issue."

He also talked long and hard about what he called "this fact: what the much-criticized tax increase of 1993 did for cutting the federal deficit and strengthening the country's economic health. It paved the way for the balanced budget agreement this year, and the tax cuts we can now afford."

Another underestimated feature of the budget, he said, is money targeted to cities, instead of to governors and states, to encourage employers to hire those who have recently been cut from the welfare rolls. The Vice President's staff wants to be sure that Mr. Gore's active involvement in that plan isn't one more underestimated feature: they remind reporters of recent meetings between top mayors and the Vice President to craft this plan.

As senators, members of Congress, and the President himself jockey to take credit for the new budget, so must the Vice President.

By getting actively involved in anything at all, Gore has already departed from the traditional role of the Vice President. He has been a major player in most of the administration's key initiatives, and is one of the President's most influential advisers.

He hungers for his party's presidential nomination in the year 2000.

To position himself advantageously, then, Al Gore has had to dance the most delicate steps of a self-promoting macarena, neither calling too much attention away from his boss, nor allowing himself to fade into the background. He can't afford to seem disloyal, but he can't afford to be ignored.

He is the President's top cheerleader. But if you listen

closely, in every rah-rah rallying cry for Numero Uno, you can hear a "Don't underestimate Number Two!"

Image is important in politics. And Gore's image as a reliable, even somewhat boring, policy maven (who gets excited about budgets) plays well—far better than his image as a Democratic party fund-raiser.

Congressional and grand jury investigations into the fund-raising muck figure to reach their climaxes later this year. Winter is coming. But this is summer. And on this sunny afternoon, Al Gore is smiling, with one eye on the budget and the other on the millennium.

OUT OF THE STARTING GATE
October 8, 1997

Arizona Republican Senator John McCain's drive for campaign finance reform is dead. But his chances for the Republican presidential nomination are alive and well.

Senate Majority Leader Trent Lott of Mississippi and House Speaker Newt Gingrich of Georgia combined to personally put the kill-shot on McCain's reform efforts.

Lott, Gingrich, and most other Republican officeholders in Washington like the money-raising system as it is. So do many Democrats. Incumbents, especially those in the majority congressional party at any given time, always like the status quo in money-raising laws. That's because they benefit the most.

So McCain's hopes for meaningful changes in the way money for politics is raised go down in flames. Just as his Navy fighter-bomber did over North Vietnam in 1967.

Incredibly, McCain survived seven years in a North Vietnamese prison. Such a man does not give up. Never.

In the hell that was his cell, he dreamed. Dreamed of sunlight and freedom.

Now he dreams of leading his country as President. He doesn't *say* that. He doesn't have to. Anyone who knows him, knows that he now burns with a hot, hard flame to have the ultimate leadership honor—and responsibility.

His desire to run, and win, the world's toughest political race is well known in Washington. Recently, around the table at a small dinner party, six of the best-known political journalists in this country were talking presidential politics. To this reporter's surprise, all of them said McCain is now a front-runner for the Republican nomination.

Hold on, you say, election day is more than *three years* away. Isn't it a little early to start covering, in horse-race terms, the campaign for the nomination, much less to start declaring front-runners?

Frankly, no. Because, like it or not, the race is on. That's why so many hopefuls are already working so hard in early-decision states such as Iowa and New Hampshire, and in the big-vote states like California and Texas.

This is what many people don't grasp: many of the important decisions about money and support are being made right now.

Presidential candidates, like pool-shooters, must constantly think of what's known around pool tables as "shape"—that is, the position you're going to be in after taking the shot just ahead.

John McCain is now playing "shape" or "position" pool. And playing it well.

For whatever, if anything, it may be worth, the early line on Republican presidential hopefuls at the moment goes like this: retired General Colin Powell is the favorite *if*—a mighty if—he really wants it and is willing to fight, all out, for it.

If you put Powell aside, former Vice President Dan Quayle is the early choice of many insiders in both parties. Surprised?

You shouldn't be. Quayle has a known name, the ability to raise unlimited sums of campaign money, and has no other job but running. He's golden with the Religious Right, and the darling of most other conservatives.

His detractors laugh, but Quayle has a serious shot, is making the most of it, and is no laughing matter in the estimation of pros in both parties.

Some of the other names being seriously discussed are Texas Governor George Bush, Senator Fred Thompson, Congressman John Kasich, and Elizabeth Dole. Previous contenders Steve Forbes, Lamar Alexander, Pat Buchanan, Pete Wilson, and Jack Kemp may still hanker for another shot.

And for those who like really long odds: Jack Welch, CEO of General Electric, is quietly being urged to have a go.

But McCain is now the hot tout in Washington, whose war heroics and gutsy stand for campaign finance reform have the smart money murmuring, "Big future."

BLUE SKIES AND GREEN LIGHTS
October 13, 1999

In a Runyonesque turn on Ecclesiastes, it's often said that "the race is not always to the swift nor the battle to the strong . . . But that *is* the way to bet it." Especially in politics.

So, you may want to note how swift and strong one—and only one—presidential candidate is running just now.

As seen from the George W. Bush for President campaign, there is nothing ahead for the Texas governor but blue skies and green lights.

In money, poll numbers, and positive press coverage, he is so far ahead of his competitors for the Republican nomination they can't even see his taillights.

And in all three of those key categories, Bush is also far ahead of both of his potential Democratic challengers for the presidency itself.

What Bush the Younger has put together is a machine. It's big, efficient, and exceptionally well lubricated, with more campaign cash than any candidate has ever banked this early. And the machine is humming along like the front-running marvel that it is.

Compared with what Bush has built, all the campaigns—Republican and Democrat—look as though they owe much to the early work of the Marx Brothers.

By any objective analysis, the Republican nomination is now clearly Bush's to lose. And that may be true of the general election as well.

And Bush knows it.

That's why he and his large staff are running with such confidence, which is maddening his opponents, frustrating and confounding them to a degree seldom if ever seen so soon in a race.

The runaway is of such proportions that many observers of all political persuasions are saying, "If John McCain doesn't stop Bush in the New Hampshire primary next year—and maybe even if he does—the nomination is Bush's."

There are other Republicans besides McCain still in the race. It's possible one of them could yet emerge as the "stopper." But McCain's name gets mentioned the most because he is widely viewed as having the best chance of beating or coming close to Bush in New Hampshire.

One reason is McCain's war record. Another is his independence, such as bucking his party's resistance to campaign finance reform. He's also an underdog. New Hampshire voters like independent, even maverick, underdogs.

But they also like the Bushes. They delivered the knockout punch for George Bush against Bob Dole in the 1988 primary. Which is one reason the son is so confident he will beat McCain and everybody else in New Hampshire and elsewhere.

It is widely believed and may be true that only a few things can stop this Bush from winning the nomination and perhaps the presidency.

(1) Overconfidence; (2) something devastatingly secret in his past that has not yet been revealed (there is no credible evidence nor testimony anywhere right now indicating that any such thing is in his past); (3) he makes a big, really big, mistake in a debate or in some other way while campaigning.

Slim reeds to cling to for those who don't want Bush to be President.

With that in mind, two points may be worth putting into the mix. One is that overnight is a long time in politics, a week is forever. And here we are talking about a Republican nomination race that won't be decided by voters for many months. The election of a new President is still more than a year away.

The second is this: in politics, as in life, what we most expect often never occurs, and what we least expect often happens.

ARE YOU RUNNING FOR SOMETHING, MRS. PRESIDENT?
February 17, 1999

Is Hillary Clinton really going to run for the Senate? She may, but anybody who says it's a cinch, doesn't know Hillary.

She is many things, but fool is not one of them. For starters, she knows that her current high poll ratings are misleading. The First Lady has been told it's what pollsters call an "artificial high." That is, a high based far less on who she is and what she stands for politically than on admiration for a put-upon, betrayed wife and mother who has carried herself with dignity through a terrible year.

Buried beneath the high are some big negatives. She is widely viewed as too strident and too liberal by many voters, including a fairly high percentage of Democrats. Her biggest foray into public policy, proposals for health-care reform, failed badly a few years ago and may still be a burden.

None of which means she could not run and win in New York (currently the speculators' top pick for imagining a new Clinton candidacy). But any race, in any state, would threaten to be mean and nasty, with no assurance she would win, and she knows it.

She will study the situation hard and long, she'll think it through thoroughly, and she'll listen to all the arguments carefully.

Among those arguing against a Senate race for her in 2000 is James Carville. The hard-fighting Louisianan isn't everybody's favorite pit bull of a political consultant, but he is the Clintons'.

When Carville speaks, the Clintons listen. He's been to hell and back, several times, for them. And Carville is warning the First Lady that a New York Senate race will be, for her, a venomous snake pit—and that she would be foolish to descend into it.

His advice is reported to be: "If you're determined to run for the Senate, wait at least until 2002, in some other state."

Some others are giving Hillary the following argument: "If you're going to run for something in 2000, run for President, or Vice President. Or wait and see what develops. One of the two places on the Democratic national ticket may open up. If they do, you, Mrs. Clinton, should be in position to seize the opportunity and moment. If you announce for the Senate, you eliminate this possibility—and that's not smart."

There is a growing body of political thought that says the Republicans are likely to put a woman on their ticket in the next presidential race. Elizabeth Dole is the most talked about possibility, of course, as a GOP presidential or vice-presidential nominee.

If Mrs. Dole or any other woman goes on the Republican ticket when they choose first at their nominating convention in 2000, the pressure will be great on Democrats to counter. And if they have to counter, who better than Hillary?

Sure, some Democrats would say Diane Feinstein, the California senator. But would she really be better than Hillary?

So Mrs. Clinton has plenty to study and think about. You can bet that she and those close to her already are running private polls and conducting focus groups to test her potential for President, Vice-President, and senator.

Everybody around her agrees that her future is bright. But exactly what that future should be and how to get it to is not easy to figure out.

She may yet decide that a Senate race in 2000 is an important piece of it. But don't bet the trailer money on it. Too early.

Whatever she decides, all the speculation and encouragement she's received in recent days has got to feel good after a year of turbulence.

MADELEINE ALBRIGHT IS READY FOR
HER CLOSE-UP
May 21, 1997

Madeleine Albright is not only the first woman to be secretary of state. She is also our first *television* secretary of state.

One reason is that, whatever the subject, she can talk it long or talk it short—you just tell her how you want it talked. And, short sound bite or long historical soliloquy, she knows how to keep it interesting.

"Maybe that's because *I'm* so interested," she says, adding,

"I have a passion for international affairs, and I have been studying them, thinking about global issues, for a long time."

Indeed she has. She got to be secretary of state the old-fashioned way: she earned it. She went back to college while she was still rearing her three children, working for advanced degrees in international studies in between making family meals and going to PTA meetings. At the same time, she worked in the trenches for every Democratic campaign since Lyndon Johnson.

She ran coffee, solicited campaign contributions, wrote speeches and position papers for candidates high and low. All the while, she studied television, too. Closely.

This came to mind during a recent interview with her. She was off-camera, waiting for our crew to change videotapes.

"It is critical to this country, critical to me, that the American public's interest in foreign policy does not flag or fail in the last years of the twentieth century. We can't afford to have that happen," she said.

"And television is key. Newspapers are important, so are magazines. But if the great mass of Americans are to be engaged in our decisions as a nation—as they must—then television exposure of the issues is absolutely vital."

For this role, she seems to be the right woman in the right job at the right time.

We have had television presidents. John Kennedy was the first. Starting with him, in every presidential race, the candidate who was the better television performer has won. Not all of them were especially good on television. But all of the winners were better than their opponents on the tube. Kennedy, Reagan, and Clinton all have been so good at it that they became known as television Presidents.

Now comes the first television secretary of state.

She bursts into the room and faces the camera all blue-eyed, smiling, and brimming with energy. Any room. Any camera. She lights up the room and cuts through on-screen. The woman has the ability to dominate any landscape she occupies, including a television studio. She has genuine presence, a kind of physical charisma—always a useful asset on television (and a necessary one in other fields such as acting or preaching).

One of her underestimated assets on television is her voice. The timbre of it is excellent, clear and crisp. It exudes confidence and authority. Communications schools struggle to teach such speaking skills, but Albright's confidence and authority are born of homework, knowledge, and her years as a teacher.

Henry Kissinger oozed confidence and authority. Before Madeleine Albright, he was the closest we had to a television secretary of state. But as a manager of the medium, Kissinger was not in Albright's league, not even close. Kissinger was a master builder of his own image. He is in the history books mainly for his dealings with China.

Albright is already assured a place in history as the first woman and first television secretary of state.

How far, if at all, she goes beyond that may depend on how she deals with China. Her television efforts to rally support for President Clinton's trade policies with the Chinese are a key early test.

Albright continues to be good television, although she gets less airtime than she used to. Ironically, one reason was a television appearance: the disastrous February 18, 1998, "town hall meeting" in Columbus, Ohio. Albright, National Security Adviser Sandy Berger, and Defense Secretary Bill Cohen tried to lay out the administration's policy toward Iraq for a program carried by the cable network CNN. But instead of rallying public support at a tough time in U.S.-Iraqi relations, they got flustered by a few protesters in the vast auditorium at Ohio State University. Television cameras magnified their discomfort, and the meeting was judged a public relations disaster.

The entire administration's enthusiasm cooled notably for most televised events.

Compounding Albright's television trouble was a new division of duties: Berger and then-Treasury Secretary Bob Rubin were designated point men on Asia; Albright became identified with Iraq, Russia, the Balkans, and the Middle East. Rightly or wrongly, she began to get mixed notices in each of these policy areas. Her television opportunities also began to dry up.

This irritated her no end, not least because she thinks her policies are criticized unfairly. But, as of this writing, America's first television secretary of state isn't broadcasting as widely as she once did.

BILL COHEN DOES HIS HOMEWORK
May 7, 1997

It's Saturday afternoon in Washington. The secretary of defense is at home. He lives in a small apartment with his wife and a dog, Lucky. They wish he would watch the basketball play-offs on television.

William Cohen played college basketball. He played well, well enough to try out for the Boston Celtics. Even now, at age fifty-six, he has a deadly long jump shot.

But this Saturday afternoon, his mind isn't on basketball. It rarely is anymore. He's worrying. Doing homework. And imagining.

Cohen has an unusually vivid imagination. He's both an accomplished novelist and poet. When's the last time the world saw a defense secretary who could say the same?

Right now he's imagining a leaner, stronger American defense. "Not more," he explains. "Less—but better. Better for the near term, to deal with present dangers such as Iran and North Korea. Better for the midterm," in case China's military capabilities become a danger, for example. "And better for the long term, for whatever threats may develop far beyond the horizon in the twenty-first century."

He believes in preparedness, even when threats aren't obvious. As the old saying goes, "You trust your mother, but you cut the cards." But he insists you don't have to be big to be prepared.

There's been no consensus about defense spending in this country since the early 1980s, when most Americans agreed we had cut too much, too fast in the wake of the Vietnam War. Can Cohen lead Americans to a new consensus on defense needs in the 1990s, a new unity on defense policy? Now is the hour. A national debate is brewing over defense dollars. So is one brutal political fight.

This is what he's worrying about this sunny Saturday afternoon.

Cohen's blue eyes are weary. His athletic shoulders sag. Too many long plane rides. Too much catching it from all sides in cut-and-thrust arguments over the defense budget.

But he brightens when this reporter asks if he's seen the President lately. Turns out he and the President have been spending more time together, more often, than most people know. While the defense secretary refuses to talk in any detail about his conversations with the President, he says that, generally, they're pondering, "Should the Pentagon be turned into a triangle? Or, when it comes to further reduction in what America spends for defense, should we cut out some of the tail but not the tooth?

"That is," he explains, "can we now, in the post–Cold War era, afford to make more big cuts in what the nation spends on defense? Can we afford not to? Or, should we pay for a more moderate course—trim but not slash, concentrating more on reducing overhead and getting increased value for dollar, less on reduction of forces and weapons systems?"

The secretary, a Republican, wants the moderate course.

The President, a Democrat, agrees. Now they have to sell it. Build first public, then congressional, support for it.

It won't be easy. The secretary served Maine on Capitol Hill for a quarter-century. He knows that no member of Congress wants a base closed in his or her district. Yet to meet the goal, more must be closed. No state or town wants weapons systems built in their area to be pruned, much less eliminated. And so it goes.

In these happy, prosperous, peaceful times, Cohen isn't sure he can sell his defense plans. But now he's the point man, the set-shot shooter in a new offensive to build consensus.

So, as the basketball play-offs unfold, he won't be watching. He'll be spending more weekends indoors, doing his homework, and imagining.

Despite Cohen's best efforts, real defense spending for preparedness has been slashed, not just trimmed. After this column appeared, Republicans and Democrats alike overrode many of his recommendations, most notably his drive for more base closings. Neither has he been able so far to build a new national consensus for stronger defense. Cohen doesn't complain. He simply says, "I'll keep trying."

THE WEARY WARRIOR
September 8, 1999

WASHINGTON, D.C.—Retired U.S. Army General Barry McCaffrey looks tired as he drops into a chair in his flag-draped office.

He is no longer the dashing, brilliant officer who led the 24th Mechanized Division to victory in the Gulf War.

McCaffrey was forty-eight then, in his prime as an American fighting man, hardened on the battlefields of Vietnam, and confident that the quick-striking force he had trained would distinguish itself in the offensive against Iraqi armor.

And it did.

But in the here and now of 1999, in the bruising pit of Washington politics, that has all faded into the mists of far away and long ago.

McCaffrey's fifty-seven now, dressed not in desert camouflage fatigues, but in his Inside the Beltway attire: dark blue suit, power tie. Of medium height and build, he is still trim, and moves with the confident grace of an aging warrior—one who has faced death and survived.

There is still a quickness to his hazel eyes, darting about, sizing up situations and people in a hurry. But there is also a tiredness.

And why wouldn't there be? He's in politics now, the "Drug Czar" in what's called "The Drug War."

But it's become much more a game of who can get credit for what and who can score political points against his opponents than a war against drug lords and drug use.

And McCaffrey has been taking some heavy shots. Republicans criticize him for being "too slow to learn what's really important and what's effective, and too slow to act on it when he does learn," as one in Congress recently told this reporter.

The specific reference was to the worsening situation in Colombia, but the quote was meant to apply to McCaffrey's tenure overall. (He took the drug-fighting job in 1996.)

Democrats criticize him for "hotdogging," as one of them with near-Cabinet rank put it after McCaffrey recently suggested it might take a fast new billion-dollar commitment to save Colombia.

While Republican Congressman Dan Burton scoffed that this is "a classic case of suggesting too little, too late," some Democrats privately complained that "McCaffrey went outside of channels and appeared to undercut Secretary of State Madeleine Albright" by going public with his new position.

In our interview, McCaffrey brushed aside all such criticism. He doesn't claim to have been right all of the time. He does point to some successes, such as reducing drug production with vigorous offenses in Bolivia and Peru. And what his staff calls "vastly improved" drug awareness and education in the U.S.

"We need to spend less time on partisan politics and more on the threat," McCaffrey says. "It's not important who criticizes whom for what. What's important is that drug abuse kills fifty-two thousand Americans a year. And that drug abuse overwhelms our criminal justice system, accounting for 50 to 80 percent of all people behind bars. And that a narco-guerrilla movement is threatening to destabilize Colombia and the surrounding region."

His tired eyes become narrower and show signs of flashing as he says this. There is a sudden burst of energy. For the rest of the interview, in word, body language, and look of the eyes, he works to convey that while he may be a weary warrior, he intends to soldier on.

But in the knowledge that he will continue to take fire from politicians in both parties as cries of "Who lost the drug war?" grow louder. And in the belief that the war can still be won if he, and we, steadfastly refuse to give up and move swiftly to a real, sustained offensive.

DAN BURTON: SOFT WALK, BIG STICK
September 22, 1999

One of the most powerful people in Washington is not among the best known. He's Dan Burton, Republican congressman from Indianapolis.

You may have heard of him, may remember something about him, because of his scathing criticism of President Clinton during the impeachment mess, and his consistent lambasting of Attorney General Janet Reno.

Like any effective politician, Burton knows the value of publicity. But unlike most politicians, he also knows the difference between publicity and news. Lately he's been making a lot of news. He is spearheading Republican efforts to reopen congressional investigations into the deadly fire at the Koresh compound outside Waco, Texas, and he is helping lead the effort to defeat the narco-guerrillas in Colombia and throughout northern South America and Panama.

Burton's also holding hearings and demanding answers as to why President Clinton recently granted clemency to members of a Puerto Rican terrorist group. Then, too, he is leveraging his power to have the National Cancer Institutes, the National Institutes of Health, and the Federal Drug Administration pay more attention to "alternative medicine." And he's raising tough questions about the wisdom of some vaccines given to infants and young children.

His power to do these things flows from his chairmanship of the House Government Reform and Oversight Committee. This dull, vague title is one reason his power isn't more recognized. Another is that Burton, unlike so many among House leaders, spends more time doing than he does talking.

But the Clinton White House recognizes his power. That's why they fear him, grudgingly respect him, and detest him.

In a recent interview in his committee's sprawling office space, Burton was relaxed and smiling. He can be fierce and unrelenting when cross-examining some hostile witness before his committee, but he is generally a friendly, garrulous type. That's why he keeps getting reelected back home in Indiana. That and his ability to deliver, big time, for his district.

"Face of a choir boy, heart of an assassin," is the way one high-ranking Clinton administration official once described him to your reporter.

"They say that because I'm effective," is Burton's chuckling response.

He is sixty-one, a tall, lean man with gray hair and hazel eyes.

About Waco, he asks, "Exactly what were U.S. military personnel doing there and who authorized whatever they did?"

On the narco-guerrilla movement that is spreading from Colombia to nearby countries, he says flatly, "The Clinton administration has been derelict." Especially, he says, in not giving the Colombia National Police helicopters and other high-tech weapons.

As for the Clinton pardons: "I don't know why they were given. I do know the American people are entitled to know."

When it comes to the medical establishment's disdain for "alternative medicine," his view is that he simply doesn't want taxpayer-funded research to be "closed-minded about the possibilities."

Vaccines for children? He doesn't argue much with present practices, but as with growing numbers of parents and grandparents, he has lots of questions but—so far—few answers.

What motivates him in these medical areas is that his wife of thirty-six years, Barbara, was diagnosed with breast cancer five years ago, and one of his grandchildren is autistic. The first spurred his interest in "alternative medicine," the second his concern about some early-childhood vaccines.

Partly because he is so openly partisan, Burton has many enemies. But love him or hate him, it is a mistake to underestimate his power.

Around Washington it's potent. And, unlike so many in Congress, he knows how to use it. Because of that you'll be hearing a lot more about him between now and the next year's national elections.

DEFAULT LIES NOT IN OUR STARS
September 22, 1995

The Republicans thundered into a two-house majority in the 1994 election, waving the Contract with America and elevating Georgia Congressman Newt Gingrich to the Speaker's chair. Suddenly pundits were openly questioning the "relevancy" of the presidency in general, and Bill Clinton in particular. Gingrich and his "Republican Revolution" looked unstoppable.

During the next budget negotiations, the Republicans tried to get the President to bow to their will. Their second tactic, a government shutdown, turned into a public relations disaster when it was learned that Gingrich had been bitter toward the President over the seating arrangements during a flight on Air Force One. What had been political (and possibly revolutionary) came to look petty and personal, and Bill Clinton was miraculously relieved of any obligation to surrender without a fight. His latest comeback began.

The first sign of trouble brewing came a few months before the shutdown, when a congressman from Texas revealed just how Republicans in Congress intended to force the President to do their will. The first tactic wasn't to be a shutdown of the government, it was to be a default on all the county's debts.

And even with Gingrich now gone and Clinton on his way out, these budget tie-ups seem to have become an annual tradition, a yearly parade of partisan politics at their worst. In 1999, Congress and the White House kicked off the U.S. government's fiscal millennium almost two months late due to their posturing.

The Republican party in Congress is threatening to send the United States of America into default on its debts for the first time in history.

The threat is real. Congress has the power to do this. Republicans now control both houses of Congress. And the Republicans' majority leader in the House, Richard Armey of Texas, has spelled out the threat in the past twenty-four hours: either President Clinton agrees to the Republican agenda in deciding how budget money is to be spent, or the Republican-controlled Congress may refuse to extend the nation's ability to borrow money to meet its bills. This would mean that, for the first time in all of its history, this nation would not be able to pay its bills. The United States would be in default.

Third- and fourth-world countries, of course, do default on debts from time to time. The United States has *never* done so.

Armey is a close confidant and ally of House Speaker Newt Gingrich. The idea behind his threat is for the Republican leadership to revive its agenda, forcing President Clinton to agree to what Republicans insist are spending priorities, and forcing him to give more ground in negotiation for a new budget. The President has said that he has already given all the ground he can give in good conscience on points such as help for the elderly and the poor. He also says that Republicans really want to *cut* such programs in order to finance tax cuts for the wealthy. Republicans argue that none of this is true. It is their claim that *they* have given more ground, that they *are* trying to help the elderly and the poor, and that their tax cuts would benefit more Americans than the very rich.

What is new now is the threat. How real the threat is taken by the world could affect interest rates, and such things as home mortgage loans tied to interest rates. It is President Clinton's contention that even threatening such an unprecedented, historic move demonstrates how "radical" (his word) the Republican Congress has become under Speaker Gingrich.

The Republicans view this as nonsense. They insist that

what the President considers "radical," most Americans actually favor—and that Mr. Clinton is simply trying to hold back a tide whose time has come.

GRIDLOCK . . . AND SERVICE
November 13, 1995

Yesterday was the New York City Marathon, hours of grueling footwork over miles of well-pounded pavement. The Marathon forces other kinds of traffic (cars, trucks, and pedestrians) to get rerouted, and the results can include some pretty hairy-scary gridlock.

There is this to be said about the Marathon, though: at least you can be sure that, one day out of the year, *some* kind of traffic will be moving in New York.

That's more than you can say for Washington, where legislative gridlock often makes New York streets look like the Indianapolis Speedway. The latest locking of the capital grids is the new budget, caught between the President and the Congress, with the possible result of a government shutdown starting tomorrow.

No matter what anyone says, this gridlock is a two-way street, Democrat and Republican. You may ask: didn't most of these guys, in Congress and in the White House, campaign on promises to *avoid* just this kind of gridlock? Wasn't gridlock the thing Americans were most irritated by? (Well, that and the lingering suspicion that our tax dollars weren't buying what they ought to.)

There *is* a legitimate difference of philosophical opinion buried somewhere in the dispute. Newt Gingrich and the Republicans want a federal government that is smaller, cheaper, and gives more power to individual states. Bill Clinton and the

Democrats are struggling to defend programs they believe the American people *don't* want to see reduced.

The shutdown isn't much of a threat: most services will still be provided, from postal delivery to air traffic control. So what's really going on isn't philosophical debate. It's political point-scoring. "If our programs don't go through," each side claims, "then it's the other guys' fault, not ours." Both sides seem to feel that finger-pointing is safer, and certainly easier, than compromise.

We are reminded that there are other ways to serve your country. America observes Veterans Day this weekend, honoring the men and women who put their lives on the line to defend this country and its freedoms. The risks and sacrifices they faced, from Normandy to Inchon, from Danang to Kuwait City, tend to put things into perspective.

Our veterans offered the last full measure of devotion to the service of their country.

Our politicians today are offering . . . well, maybe you'll have to explain it to me.

VIETNAM WINS: CLINTON LIFTS
THE TRADE EMBARGO
February 3, 1994

My experience as a correspondent during the Vietnam War is one I'll never shake—and don't care to shake. To this day I am moved by the commitment and service I saw on the part of so many American men and women in the field. By far the great majority of these Americans were models of devotion to their country, belief in freedom, a desire to help others.

As a result, I am—let's be honest—biased in favor of

*the men and women who served in Vietnam. My hackles
rise whenever their integrity is questioned (especially by
those who didn't see them in action), when their interests
seem to be threatened (especially for those who can no
longer speak for themselves), when their memory is
shown anything less than total respect.*

*I was stunned when President Clinton lifted the trade
embargo on Vietnam, February 3, 1994. Although I later
revised these remarks and submitted them to* National
Review, *this draft, written in haste and broadcast on radio the day the White House announced the news, re-
flects the rawness of my feelings so well that I have
included it instead of the perhaps more polished version
that appeared in William Buckley's magazine a few days
later.*

President Clinton may have lost the election today. Should
Bill Clinton be nominated again and run in 1996, and should
he lose, he may—we all may—look back on this day as the
day he lost.

Reason: lifting the trade embargo on Vietnam. This is a
renege, a flat-out welsh on a campaign promise. He gave his
word that he would not lift the trade embargo until and unless
there was a full, good-faith accounting for Americans still
missing in action from the war. We are still waiting for the
accounting.

A little background: families of men still missing in Vietnam
were furious, especially after President George Bush appeared
(at least appeared to many of the families) to have given them
short shrift and double-talk at a meeting.

Then-candidate Bill Clinton took full advantage. In his drive
to unseat President Bush, that's when he made his promise.

Today, he broke the promise.

As North Vietnam sees it, they were victorious in the war
and now, once again victorious. That is how *they* see it, how
it is being trumpeted in Hanoi.

When your reporter was in Hanoi a few months back, with retired U.S. General Norman Schwarzkopf, the headlines were: U.S. WILL CAVE ON TRADE EMBARGO. When I asked about that, a fully confident Vietnamese government official told me, "We had more determination and patience than America did during the fighting, and we have more about this. Yes, America will cave—and soon." He smiled. When I asked why he was so confident, he smiled again. "Money," he replied. "Your businessmen want the money. And money moves America."

Your reporter left the room. I admit it, I was mad.

Today, that seems a long, long time ago.

Today, the deal is done. Vietnam gets what it wants. And the headlines in Hanoi must be: U.S. CAVES ON TRADE EMBARGO.

As one reporter contemplates all of this, he wonders: has it occurred to President Clinton, or to any of those around him who advised him so vigorously to lift this embargo—has it occurred to them to go, tonight, to the Wall?

It is only a short walk from the White House. The Wall, the Vietnam Memorial, where more than fifty-eight thousand American names are carved in the garden of stone.

Only the President can answer whether he has kept faith with those who gave the last full measure of devotion, those who sacrificed their valor and their lives in a cause their country and its leaders told them at the time was important. They may have gone to the wrong war, but they went for the right reasons. And so did those still officially listed as missing.

It might mean nothing, and then again it might mean something, if the President underscored that he and the nation understand that—on this day, of all days.

President Clinton's policy toward Vietnam didn't seem to have any noticeable effect on his reelection campaign. But U.S. Senator John McCain, a former prisoner of war in Vietnam (see page 132), took issue with this article, saying he agreed with the President's policy. "It's time to move forward," McCain told me.

ANTI-SEMITISM AND
THE CLINTON DOCTRINE
January 27, 1993

In practice, President Clinton has preferred to call "constructive engagement" the policies based on his philosophy of economic and political interdependence, which I identified as his "doctrine" very early in his administration. Either way, he hasn't been consistently successful in applying it. And even if, in Germany, the old demons of fascism are not dancing quite so boldly now as they were in 1993, the dance continues all across Europe, from Moscow to Marseilles.

You've seen the pictures from Germany: Jews and immigrants beaten up, burned out, killed. Skinheads. Swastikas. Nazi salutes. Cries of: *Ausländer raus! Foreigners get out!* Chilling images from the *present*. It wasn't supposed to happen again. But it is.

The apparent resurgence of anti-Semitism, ethnic hatred, and neo-Nazism in Germany in recent months has concerned a lot of people in the U.S. Not least because it could be happening here, too.

In an interview last week, I asked President Clinton if he'd done any thinking about Germany's renewed troubles. His prompt response: "Yes." Part of the problem, he said, was that the young people (who he believes are at the core of the movements in Germany) are too young to remember the suffering, the ugliness, the inhumanity of the Third Reich.

Clinton also linked ethnic division over there to ethnic division over here. He said that last spring he'd been to Brooklyn to visit a synagogue that had been vandalized. The people in Brooklyn believed the ethnic divisions in their neighborhood were caused by a declining American economy, diminished prospects, and rising insecurity.

In Germany, too, President Clinton believes that economics lie at the heart of the trouble. He told me, "Bringing in the East cost them a lot more than they thought it would." He said refugees and job losses in the East have made young Germans insecure; so "they're glomming onto something terrible."

Clinton suggests that the solution may be the same for ethnic tension abroad and at home. He proposes "a new era of concentrated support for democracy and freedom *and* economic growth" for Germany, for the rest of Europe, and for Japan. If that sounds familiar, it's because that's what he proposed for the United States.

Remember that the first round of German Nazism exploited the economic weakness brought about by the Great Depression. The people wanted to blame someone: Hitler provided the targets.

Of course, talking about the economy is largely what got Clinton elected, but it seems clear that the new President honestly believes a strong economy can alleviate almost any problem in any society.

Historically, Presidents have resorted to doctrines of force of arms or government spending in the name of problemsolving. So far, the doctrine of economic strength, in this country and abroad, seems to be the Clinton Doctrine.

He could do worse.

AN OPEN LETTER, OPENLY IGNORED
December 22, 1992

*Need I really point out that, if Bill Clinton had fol-
lowed my advice, and if it had turned out to be bad advice, I wouldn't be reprinting this essay now?*

Dear President-elect Clinton:

I know you're getting a lot of advice these days (*The New
York Times* has, for the first time in its history, started printing
an advice column—but it's an advice column for you alone).
Well, get used to it. Advice for the President is one thing you
can be sure everybody has.

To tell the truth, I've got some advice for you myself.

1. *Don't get photographed smoking any more cigars.* In
   fact, give up cigars altogether. They make you—they
   make anybody—look like Edward G. Robinson in *Little
   Caesar,* and they'll make trouble for you at home. Wives
   and cigars are not a happy mix. (Don't ask how I know
   this: just take my word for it.)
2. *Give up golf.* H. L. Mencken once said, "Never trust a
   journalist who plays golf." The same rule applies to presidents. People don't trust golf. No matter how humble its
   origins, its intentions, or its actuality, it *looks* elitist. A
   caddy looks like a servant, period. Manicured lawns and
   freshly swept sand traps have about as much to do with
   the life led by the average Americans as do jousts and
   mead. Those little bumper cars make grown men look
   silly. And the clothes would better suit your trusted adviser Ronald McDonald. Mr. President-elect, give up golf.
3. *Get a dog.* I say this sympathetically, because I've got a
   daughter myself, a daughter who likes cats—but get a
   dog. You don't have to get rid of Socks, even if Chelsea

would let you. It is true that cats and dogs *can* live harmoniously together. They've done it at my house. If they do it at the White House, it will make great political symbolism. But beyond that, you *need* a dog. I know that your pollsters and advisers are telling you not to worry, that surveys show that there are more cat owners than dog owners in America, but there are a few things you need to keep in mind about that.

First, it isn't true. Second, it wouldn't matter if it were true. In this case, image is everything. Dogs say . . . *America*. Cats say . . . *France*.

And remember that Socks the Cat will not come bounding up happily to see you when you want to change the subject at a press conference.

Please bear in mind, Mr. President-elect, that this is the rare piece of advice you've had in weeks from anybody who doesn't want to be adjunct undersecretary of anything.

Chapter 4

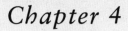

TRIBUTES

THE LAST GRANDMOTHER
September 5, 1985

She sits out there along Pin Oak Creek, out where not so long ago buffalo literally roamed and Sam Houston rode. When there's no moon and the wind's up a bit at night, they say you can sometimes still hear the clippety-clop of Sam Houston's horse. That's what some of them say. You ask Granny, and she just smiles.

All four of my own grandparents are long gone; three of my wife's are. That leaves only Granny, the only granny in the family now. She doesn't see or hear as well as she once did, but she can still hear the murmur of the cottonwood trees, and she still occasionally sees a bobcat scamper across a clearing.

She is—what? Somewhere in her early to mid-nineties. Still insists on living alone out there in the country, miles from anywhere and anybody. She was born in that house, long before Teddy Roosevelt was ever President. Her mother and father died there. All of her children were born there. She has never lived anywhere else and has no intention of doing so. She lives out there on her own, by herself, doing her chores, running her little store, way out there in the country and way back there in time.

She now has a wagon-train face with the kind of steady gaze that tells you in an instant that she doesn't lie and doesn't tolerate those who do. She is delicate as a rose but tough as iron.

Some years back, two young toughs with beer on their breaths and theft in their hearts threatened her. She cracked one with an ax handle, wheeled, and asked the other if he wanted some of that, too. He didn't. They left. She was in church the next Sunday, of course, asking for forgiveness and for more humility and grace.

For those and a thousand other reasons I always like to see her. She is one of the constants in my life, in all our lives, those of us lucky to know her. She smiles. She loves. She endures. Over the years and over the miles you just knew she would always be there.

But this time, for the first time, it hit me and soaked in. She will not always be there. She is fragile and getting more so, and she knows it. She accepts that. She is not afraid. Fear of anything or anybody, save God, just isn't in her. She accepts it—her increasing fragility and vulnerability—and she is worried. She is so proud and so independent, so fiercely determined to make it on her own.

But out there, alone, she is wondering, wondering whether she can make it through another winter. Should she chance it or move to town? We shall soon see. In the meantime, I am wondering. Sooner or later, if not this winter, then sometime, Granny will no longer be with us.

The last grandmother will be gone. What will we do?

She was reared different from me. Her character was constructed of tougher materials than mine. Everything she has—food, shelter, freedom, life—is hard and freshly won. She knows the value of what she has.

She has tried, in her quiet way, to teach us many things: how to churn butter, how to make biscuits from scratch, how to rear a loving child. Now it's time for us to pass on her lessons to our own children and grandchildren.

And suddenly there are so many things I realize I don't know. Granny makes it all look so simple: follow a few steps to achieve the desired results. But I stumble along the path. I leave out the most important part whenever I try to tell one of her stories. When I sing her songs, I forget the verse and go straight to the chorus.

I see the flash of Granny's pioneer fierceness in her great-granddaughter's eyes, but I don't know how to coax it forth and cultivate it, any more than I can coax and cultivate lightning. Is Robin supposed to find her core values and character for herself? Or am I supposed to teach her? How can I live up to the standard Granny set? It is the peculiar panic of parenthood.

Granny doesn't seem to worry. Her love for us gives her faith in us: that's one of her values, maybe first among them. She believes we'll turn out fine. Her generation built this country and this century, and you can't do that without confidence.

She smiles and gives me a little pat on the hand. She faces the sunset with eyes bright. I see the coming of the night, but Granny is already thinking of the dawn.

Granny Goebel passed away in 1992, leaving a Texas-sized hole in our hearts.

REMEMBERING JOHN
July 21, 1999

Don't let it be forgot,
That once there was a spot.
For one brief shining moment that was known
As Camelot.

His mother sang it to him when he was a baby. She loved the Arthurian legend and loved the musical based on it that was so popular at the time.

The mental picture and the music now haunt as we think of another Kennedy gone. Another piece of America gone.

You don't have to like the Kennedys, personally or politically, to feel a tug at the heart as the bells toll for young John. You can damn them, praise them, or just say you don't know what to think about the family, as a clan and as a political force. But you know, down deep, that this is a family that has epitomized many positive characteristics that we, as a people, treasure as quintessentially American:

Faith, resolve, refusal to shrink from challenges, and eyes always on the far frontier and the future.

And this time, as another Kennedy goes, the loss is deeply personal, profoundly our own. Because for so many, John F. Kennedy, Jr., was America's son.

That is what John became, one dark November day in 1963, when, not quite three years old, he suddenly lost his father.

The child, so young and so brave, captured our hearts.

We took him in, as one of our own and watched him grow over the years into a bright, articulate, handsome young man trying—as all sons must—to find his way, to make something of himself, out on his own.

A young man any one of us would be proud to call "son."

Among the most poignant and unforgettable images in the American family album is of the son saluting the father as his mother, wearing a long, black veil, wept behind him.

From that moment, the son carried the burden and the honor of being a symbol.

The country saw something profound in the child. He had lost a father. A nation had lost its leader. But something more was lost, and we knew it. A sense of security, of innocence.

In young John Kennedy, America saw something of itself—an orphaned nation reflected in the wide eyes of an orphaned child. And as this little boy tried to find his way out of that dark time, so did we.

Now, as with his father before him, we can only imagine what might have been. He gave some hints to a friend, who wondered what song JFK Jr. would pick for his theme if he ever became President.

John's answer: "Chimes of Freedom," by Bob Dylan.

In the song, Dylan pays tribute to the dispossessed, the lonely, and the lost. The chimes of freedom toll for silent seekers of truth and love, and for ". . . each unharmful gentle soul misplaced inside a jail."

The chimes we now hear are tolling in grief.
The flash has faded into darkness.
America's son is lost and gone forever.

REMEMBERING MARTIN
April 7, 1999

AUSTIN, TEXAS—Spring has come to the Texas hill country. The sun seems to grow a little warmer every day, and wildflowers turn every hillside into a tapestry any king would covet.

Yet our hearts are heavy.

This Easter we lost my wife's father. Martin Goebel finished only the fifth grade, in a one-room schoolhouse attached to the church where his father and his father's father had worshiped.

But he was smart. Smart enough to fix or build anything mechanical: farm implements, cars, heavy machinery.

He was a builder and a dreamer, enough of both to start half a dozen small manufacturing businesses and make them successful enough to make a living and to provide employment for hundreds of other people over the years.

He eventually lost all but one of his tiny factories. First one thing, then another. But he seldom complained. When he lost a business, he'd just dream anew and build another one.

In his own shade-tree mechanic, baling-wire, and duct-tape way, he was an entrepreneur before the word became fashionable.

He had a glint in his eye, a pioneer gaze that seemed to take in the whole horizon at once, and maybe saw a little bit beyond the horizon, too.

You can still see that glint in the eyes of his daughters. I saw it in Jeannie's eyes, and I married her.

We buried Martin in the cemetery behind his little church. As the steeple bell rang, a passing train nearly drowned it out.

Martin would've liked that. He once earned his living repairing locomotives, often making the replacement parts himself.

He was a big man, well over six feet and two hundred pounds. He was filled with outsized passions and prejudices, not all of them admirable. That's the way with most of us. But Martin was never shy with his opinions.

"Don't confuse me with the facts," he once thundered, "I've already made up my mind."

On another occasion, he created a stir in a restaurant by loudly announcing to a waitress, "Young lady, salad isn't FOOD. Salad is what food EATS!"

Beef is what he ate. Bourbon is what he drank—no ice, no water. Straight.

Which is also how he talked. He could be counted on to give the anchorman an earful. Whether the anchorman wanted it or not.

The truth is seldom easy, least of all when it's coming from your father-in-law. But it was the only language Martin really understood.

My own parents passed away while I was still a young man, but for more than forty years, Martin obligingly acted as a kind of surrogate father for me. I was able to turn to him for comfort or honest criticism. And I always felt safe in the knowledge that he was looking out for our family.

Now I will have to learn what it means to be a grown-up without him.

For years Martin and his widow, Hilda, kept our family connected to the small-town Texas that bore us, but that is fading away.

Martin and Hilda reared their daughters—and oversaw the rearing of their grandchildren and great-grandchildren—to be citizens of a small town, no matter where they went. To look out for their neighbors. To work hard. To appreciate life's blessings.

Now it's up to us who survive, to keep passing those lessons along.

In my lifetime, I've circled the globe a hundred times. I've walked and talked with presidents and princesses, with tribal chiefs and tenors.

I've looked in them for the qualities I admired in him. But I never met the match of Martin Goebel.

THE PRINCESS OF PIN OAK CREEK
October 6, 1999

Among the oaks and willows along the riverbank where she was born, a great American lady is fading away.

They have taken Hilda Kasper Goebel home to die. By the time you read this she may be gone.

She had hoped to see the twenty-first century. The doctors say that is not to be. Too bad, for she still had so much to teach about who and what we are, where and what we've come from.

Beginning with her faith. Like a rock. She was taught from infancy to fear God but not death. She believed it and lived it.

She lived her life believing no ill could harm her, no foe alarm her, in the hollow of God's hand.

Now the pale horse and his rider have come. She does not fear him. Although she rarely speaks now, she is sometimes awake. And her blue eyes tell you: I hurt but I am not afraid. She still believes, and will to the end. (For her it is a beginning, the beginning of a whole new life everlasting.)

Hers is what's sometimes called "that oldtime religion." Even as she endures a slow, agonizing death, she clings to what is for her, literally, the Rock of Ages.

She was born in 1913 on a farm, at a time when many if not most Americans still were farmers. She picked cotton and milked cows all of her early life. At first, she was schooled at home, mostly from the Bible. Her parents did not speak English at home. Neither did she until the local Lutheran church opened a one-room school.

She never finished high school. Too much work to do on the farm, and besides, nobody around her then thought it important for a woman to have very much education. But she was smart. Very. And her proudest moment came when, at the age of seventy-two, she earned her high-school-equivalency diploma.

Her beauty, too, was a legend in the county. Only four feet eleven inches and never weighing more than one hundred pounds, her figure, her face, and her gentle manner made her pretty all of her life.

In her prime, she was an uncrowned Miss America, the Princess of Pin Oak Creek. Even into her eighties, people marveled at her physical beauty and the inner peace that enhanced it.

As a child, she had taught herself to play the family's heirloom organ from the old country. Later, for decades, she played the church organ. Every Sunday.

Through wars, depressions, family tragedies and triumphs, she was a constant. She read her Bible, played her organ, sang her hymns, and in a soft but steady voice gave prayers, comfort, and encouragement whenever and wherever she could.

Nobody can remember her saying anything unkind about anybody.

While still in her teens, she had married her childhood sweetheart from the farm next door. He died earlier this year. And when he died, something seemed to go out of her. Her reason for living.

And now she is in the midst and mists of crossing the river to join him. Her children, grandchildren, and great-grandchildren are all around her, weeping as she goes.

So is her oldest son-in-law. I, like the others, weep not for her loss, because *she* has not lost. She is being carried home to victory. No, we weep because our faith is not as strong as hers.

We are of a different time and a different America. And, as we softly sing to her "Will the Circle Be Unbroken," we fear we know the answer.

TOUCHED BY A PRINCESS
September 6, 1997

I was honored to be asked by the London Evening Standard *to contribute to a special edition commemorating the life of Princess Diana, published the day of her funeral. The editors of the* Evening Standard *asked me to explain to the British what Diana had meant to Americans.*

Americans are said not to care much about "foreign" news. The prevailing perception is that the farther a story is from the American doorstep, the less the American audience will pay attention.

Yet for the past week my network's radio and television

news operations have been based in London, reporting on this nation's sense of loss after the death of Diana, princess of Wales. And our ratings have risen.

If numbers are what interest you, the numbers prove it: Americans do care about this story. But you don't need statistics to tell you the truths of the heart.

Back home, Americans are watching—and weeping. Because to us, there was nothing "foreign" about Princess Diana.

In America, as in Britain, Diana struck a chord. In my country, as in yours, she connected.

It wasn't just the look, the sense of style, the grace, the charm, the smile and warmth, although we appreciated those.

It was her vulnerability that spoke most clearly to Americans, and her willingness to let her vulnerability be known, to let it show and to talk about it.

When Diana came on the scene, in that storybook wedding ceremony, Americans were on the verge of rediscovering an age-old truth: the English are awfully good at theater.

We would come to accept that truth wholeheartedly within a few years, but Andrew Lloyd Webber and Emma Thompson, and all the other English theatrical exports eagerly embraced by the Americans in the eighties and nineties, only followed a trail that the princess of Wales blazed, beginning with her wedding. The royal wedding was theater, it was lavish spectacle filled with colorful characters. The royal family had put on pageants before, but not perhaps since the queen's coronation had the emotions risen so high, the feelings been shared so widely.

Diana herself made the difference. She was the reason the royal wedding became something more than all the other pageants we'd witnessed in the years before. Suddenly, here was a character at the center of this drama about whom we could care.

We may have been wrong, but we believed we recognized in Diana something of young women we knew, perhaps even something of ourselves.

When she kissed the prince on the balcony of Buckingham Palace, in front of a joyful mob, she rewrote the script with a single, slightly nervous movement. This wasn't just a choreographed national ritual designed to solemnize the production of royal heirs—this was a *wedding,* recognizable as a wedding, the sort of wedding *we* might attend.

The play was never going to be the same, and Diana's character would remain central, in the next act and in all the rest.

That may not have been what others intended, but Diana was always revolutionary.

And, although Americans sometimes forget it, we are revolutionary, too. Like it or not, we are.

A later act in the drama of Diana—her divorce—had resonance for Americans at least in part because we, too, are unsure of our position with respect to royalty. We are fascinated by royalty, we love the theater of it, and we hold the British monarchy in particular esteem since the heroism of the royal family during the Second World War. But we are decidedly uneasy when it comes to the institutions of royalty.

Diana seemed to rebel against protocol and traditions that, to most Americans, appeared unnecessarily restrictive, even unreasonable. We sensed that Diana was, in her heart, almost American in her rebellion against the Crown.

Mostly, however, Diana's divorce touched Americans because so many of us have been affected by divorce.

In our own lives, we have become almost accustomed to the accusations, the recriminations, the terrible pain, the slanders passed back and forth by "friends," and all the social battlefield that is a divorce.

Diana and Charles's separation held up a mirror to modern life—just as we are supposed to learn from the suffering of kings in a tragedy at the theater.

It was just before the separation that Diana learned to play the underdog, a role that appeals to most Americans. And she played the role the way Americans like it played: tough, with a fierce determination to survive.

Those were the days when she began showing us her vulnerability. Her tears moved us, yes. But the fact she let us see them at all was even more important, another act of rebellion.

Her tears, her frowns, her words, and gestures were tailor-made for an era when we Americans are relentlessly encouraged to "get in touch with our feelings." Diana, we felt, really did need to get in touch with her feelings, to break away from the traditional reserve of the monarchy.

She seemed very bad at reserve, incapable of holding in her true emotions, unable to disguise her real self—that is, she seemed to us just like an American.

It wasn't only her vulnerability that persuaded us. We loved to look at pictures of her when she was doing her charitable work, visiting the sick, the maimed, the abused. Her eyes spoke directly to us. She wasn't making a routine public appearance. She sincerely wanted to be helping others.

Diana was a toucher, and in touch. Look at any picture as she reaches out to a child—there is something more than sympathy in her eyes. It is communication, one that grew more profound, more expressive, with every year.

And now America has turned its eyes to Diana one last time. We have come, we radio and television networks, so that all Americans can attend the funeral of a remarkable woman, whom we may have understood imperfectly, but about whom we cared as if she were one of our own.

We won't forget her.

A POET WITH A CAMERA IN TOW
July 7, 1997

An edited version of the following essay appeared in the New York Times.

I suffered both a personal and a professional loss this July Fourth, although perhaps not quite the way you might expect.

The loss of Charles Kuralt was a personal loss, but it had nothing to do with the fact that we'd known and worked with each other for most of our adult lives. The truth is, I didn't know Charles very well—knew enough not to call him Charlie, but the Charles I knew wasn't the flesh-and-blood colleague so much as the televised Mr. Kuralt. In that sense, the personal loss I feel is one shared by millions of viewers. We knew Charles Kuralt, we liked him and listened to him, and we believed he'd listen to *us*: we began missing him the minute he signed off the air three years ago.

Contrary to appearances, Charles Kuralt was not the Sir John Falstaff of CBS News. Yes, he loved playing the *bon vivant*, and his *On the Road* crew sometimes seemed as much a band of rogues as Pistol and Bardolph and Hal. But he played that part only for a select audience—for Bernie Birnbaum, Izzy Blackmon, or Karen Beckers, for example. The rest of us could only envy their closeness, and admire from a distance Charles Kuralt's remarkable character and work. We suspected that, if only we practiced some obscure craft—if we were masters of some obscure, ancient American art, if we could whittle or play music on our teeth, or juggle cats—then we might be his friends, too.

When he came to CBS, he was the youngest reporter in the News Division. Young reporters were rare then. We were only just beginning to hire anybody who hadn't reported on—or fought in—World War II. (Nowadays it seems we hire reporters so young that we can't be sure they've *heard* of World War II.) I showed up a couple of years later, a couple of years older.

In those days, CBS News was a writer's shop. I fancied myself a writer—I'd have stayed a print reporter if I'd been a better speller—but Charles was the genuine article, a real writer, not a wannabe, not a gonnabe.

No one has ever written television news reports so well, for so long. Mostly he wrote television essays, a magical blend of word, picture, and voice. He narrated those essays at a soak-it-up pace, in a deep, rich baritone. He melded words and voice with pictures—and natural sounds, birds chirping or a father sighing—peerlessly.

Charles's essays were miniature movies, carefully scripted, filmed, and edited. They told of our life and times. They had breadth, depth, and sweep to engage the eye, ear, *and* mind.

Charles was the first correspondent to take his typewriter into the editing room regularly. "Let the film talk to you," he once told me over a beer (it was still film in those days, not videotape). "Listen to the pictures, hear what the pictures are saying, then write to them as you would write to music."

He didn't try to copy Eric Sevareid or Charles Collingwood (although one could do worse): he already had his own style. It matched his voice. It even matched his look, which, even in those days, was all wrong for television, and yet exactly right for the things he wanted to talk about.

By the end of his career, he had turned that style, that voice, that look—and that subject matter—into a package of virtues, and a quietly defiant challenge to all the so-called experts of television news. That's the root of the professional loss I feel, and one reason I kept rooting for him to come back to work, one of these days.

Charles had become the living antithesis of all the conventional wisdom about television news. He was balding at a time when the blow-dryer is acknowledged the most important piece of technical equipment in the newsroom. Perhaps he didn't defeat the conventional wisdom altogether—but despite the experts' insistence that television is all about pictures and movement, Charles put nearly equal emphasis on words, and an even greater emphasis on people and feelings.

When he went on the road, he left behind the disappointments that many of us reporters felt with our subjects. The people he interviewed hadn't cheated the government, or broken the law, or manufactured defective products. They'd baked a cherry pie, or made bricks with their bare hands, or healed the sick—and Charles admired them for it. He walked away feeling better, not worse—and we felt better, too.

On *Sunday Morning* he actually dared to talk to and about poets and painters and singers—he didn't believe that coverage of the arts should be left like hand-me-downs from the networks to PBS. He was willing to bet that some of his viewers had heard of these artists, and that the rest would want to.

At a time when the pace of television only quickens, Charles actually slowed down. (I've been told that news writers had to jettison about a quarter of the script whenever Charles subbed for me on the *CBS Evening News*—he read that much more slowly than I.)

In an era when newsrooms around the country, and at all the networks, are consciously "dumbing down," Charles was willing to gamble that his audience had read at least one book in the past month.

He was even willing to gamble on his greatest strength—his writing—and to trust his own silence at the end of every broadcast, when his camera crews would open a window onto the world of nature, and the only sounds we'd hear were birdcalls and burbling brooks.

These were dangerous gambles. I can't tell you how few voices there were telling Charles to do it his way.

But he was right. The proof is in the audience—the fiercely loyal audience who mourn him today, perhaps the last loyal audience in television news. Charles Kuralt challenged the conventional wisdom, and won.

We have been too slow picking up his challenge—maybe that's one reason he never came back to work.

But there are mornings when I am interviewing someone *I like*—whether it's Horton Foote or Willie Nelson, a teacher in Houston or a rice farmer in Huang Gong—when I am reminded that Charles Kuralt and I are members of the same profession, practitioners of the same craft, and that, as there was room for him to offer political analysis on election night, so there ought to be room for me—for all of us—to go on the road from time to time.

We will seek to avoid disappointment: we will look for the good in our subjects. We will tell the market researchers and other television geniuses to take a flying leap from time to time: we will trust ourselves. We will not talk down to our audience: we will respect them. We will try to share not only our knowledge, but our delight: the people and places and pleasures we have found in our travels.

If we are looking to pay Charles Kuralt some lasting tribute, we couldn't do better than to start right there.

A SAINT WHO KNEW WHAT SHE WANTED
September 10, 1997

CALCUTTA—When the funerals of the world's two best-known women fall just one week apart, it's tempting for a reporter covering both of them to draw comparisons. Like Princess Diana, Mother Teresa found a way to use her fame to direct public attention to her concerns. But the fact is, there is no fair comparison.

In Britain, millions mourned a tragedy in Diana's death. In India, they celebrated a spirit in Mother Teresa's life. And while Diana's was a life cut brutally short, Mother Teresa's was a life lived out fully.

For those who had the privilege to meet her, one thing was very clear about this "saint of the gutter." Mother Teresa was no otherworldly prayer-book saint. No eyes cast heavenward and hands folded primly over heart.

If Mother Teresa was a saint, and there's a good chance she'll be named one in our lifetime, then she will be a saint with eyes searching for those in need, and her sari sleeves rolled up to help.

When it came to her work with the poorest of the poor, Mother Teresa may have been humble, but she was no doormat. She built an organization with more than five hundred missions in more than a hundred countries. While other groups of nuns were shrinking, her community grew dramatically, in spite of the heavy demands the work made on her sisters. Some five thousand Missionaries of Charity carry on her work today.

Anyone who's covered her at a press conference knows she was a presence, one of those rare people whose electricity you felt in a room, even before you saw her. There was a force of moral power about her. And she wasn't hesitant to use it for the good of her work.

If popes or presidents, bishops or mayors weren't doing all they could to help that work, then the frail-looking four-foot, eleven-inch nun didn't hesitate to prod the powerful. The hospices and AIDS centers, the shelters for the abused and the abandoned that circle the world are all tributes to Mother Teresa's persuasive powers.

Early this summer, Mother Teresa went to see Rudy Giuliani, the mayor of New York City. She wanted that most precious of New York commodities, parking space. Her nuns, she explained, were having trouble visiting their AIDS patients because they couldn't find legal parking spots. "I'd do anything Mother Teresa wanted," the mayor said at the time. "If Mother Teresa wants more parking, she can have more parking." The nuns got special permits.

Make no mistake about it—for all her shelters and orphanages and food lines, Mother Teresa was no social worker. She was a Catholic nun motivated by her Christian convictions and gospel mandates. Mother Teresa never made any apologies for those beliefs. She spoke out unapologetically about her opposition to the death penalty and abortion, about her concern that affluent westerners were warehousing their aged parents in nursing homes.

Mother Teresa never watered down her message to fit her audience. She was as willing to afflict the comfortable as to comfort the afflicted, as a startled President and Mrs. Clinton discovered at a National Prayer Breakfast, when the nun moved seamlessly from family values to abortion.

But instead of turning people off, Mother Teresa's straightforward and consistent message gained her respect and even a degree of celebrity, both inside and outside her religious community.

She was one tough lady, on a mission from God.

CBS News writer Frank Devine wrote the first draft of the preceding column.

AMERICAN JOURNALISM IS A TRULY FRIENDLY PLACE
March 4, 1998

Not many people will tell you this, but Fred Friendly could be a pain in the neck.

The legendary CBS News producer and Columbia University professor, who died March 4, caught any mistake you made.

He was aided in this by the fact that he'd made plenty of mistakes of his own. While a record of fallibility didn't necessarily make him any more charitable toward those who failed, it did make it easier for him to recognize our excuse-making, rationalizations, and defenses.

Some of journalism's favorite defenses—"I'd like to see you do better!"—were completely useless against Fred. He'd been Edward R. Murrow's collaborator and producer for *See It Now, CBS Reports,* and other landmark programs, setting the standard for journalistic excellence on television. That task was all the more difficult because television was so new: there was nobody to copy, no rule-book (until they wrote it), no guide but their consciences.

Eventually, Fred became president of CBS News. One way and another, he was my boss for several years. At home or on the road, if I made a mistake, Fred would call.

In 1963, Fred called. For a documentary he was producing, I'd interviewed Judge Leander Perez, one of the last old-time segregationist powers, in his lair at Plaquemines Parish, Louisiana.

"Dammit," Fred boomed. (Sometimes he seemed to think my full name was "Dammit Rather," or "Damn" for short.) "Go back there, and do the interview again. Your questions weren't tough enough. Follow up, bore in, don't let him off the hook.

"What I'm looking at here isn't your best work. Don't you *ever* send me anything less than your *best* work." Bam. He slammed the receiver down.

Now, no matter what level you've reached in your career (and I was clover-green at the time), you haven't really practiced journalism if you haven't gone up to a notorious Southern bigot so ornery that the Pope excommunicated him, and try to explain to him that "Uh, you see, sir, my boss back in New York would like for you to sit down and do this all over again so that I can 'get tough' with you, please, sir . . ."

I wasn't the only one Fred upbraided. He became the voice of integrity for all of broadcast journalism. And, brother, his voice was *loud*.

In 1966, he resigned in protest because CBS wouldn't pre-empt soap operas for congressional hearings about the Vietnam War. But he didn't fade away.

Just when you thought you could breathe a sigh of relief, follow the herd, and go with the flow—just when you thought it was safe to go back to the waters of laziness and complacency—you found out the truth.

Fred had started teaching. At Columbia University's journalism school. Suddenly, his students were everywhere. Questioning. Analyzing. Reminding you of your principles and duties. Pointing out your mistakes. Sounding exactly like Fred.

One student, my friend Tom Bettag, is now executive producer of ABC's *Nightline*. Another friend, Mark Harrington, helped create MSNBC. They've never really stopped doing coursework for Professor Friendly's class.

Thanks to such students in newsrooms across the country, American journalism is never going to shake off Fred's influence. That is, if we're lucky.

At Columbia, Fred and his wife, Ruth, introduced the Friendly Seminars, often broadcast on public television. Policy makers and press were lined up and asked to discuss a hypothetical situation: how would you respond, for example, if the United States were under terrorist attack, Mme. Senator or Mr. Reporter?

You began by spouting all your best ethical rhetoric. But under Fred's grilling, you wound up exposing every contradiction between your ideals and your real behavior.

It was an exhausting experience (I underwent it numerous times). In an afternoon, you could clear truckloads of cant and cobwebs out of your ethical processes.

Yes, Fred could be a pain. But you had to love a guy who believed—with every bone in his body—that you were capable of doing good work, and who never stopped urging you to do even better work.

My telephone won't seem like an instrument of moral instruction, now that Fred won't be calling anymore. I'm going to miss that.

ROLE MODEL FOR A GENERATION
January 21, 1993

WASHINGTON, D.C.—The news these days is all beginnings and endings. President Bush steps down, President Clinton steps up. The word has gone forth: from the generation of "Americans born in this century, tempered by war, disciplined by a hard and bitter peace," the torch has been passed to "a new generation of Americans raised in the shadow of the Cold War."

And something else. Call it a generational milestone if you wish. Yesterday, Audrey Hepburn died.

It seems impossible. She was so young.

That look of hers—the girlish face, the deep dark eyes, the long slender waist—was the Look of a generation. For years, women starved themselves and copied her clothes—the shirt dress in *Roman Holiday,* the bohemian black stockings in *Funny Face,* the A-line dress in *Breakfast at Tiffany's.* A generation did its darnedest to look like her.

Well, every generation is permitted its folly. And for one generation, one folly was this: we concentrated on the *externals* of Audrey Hepburn. The externals were irresistible. But all the while, the *internal* Audrey Hepburn got more and more astonishing.

Audrey Hepburn never forgot her experiences in World War II. Raised in Holland, she grew up under Nazi occupation. She suffered in wartime. She almost died of malnutrition.

Years later, she rolled up her sleeves and went to work for the United Nations Children's Fund—UNICEF.

Another movie star might have treated this as a glamorous opportunity, raising money, going to fancy parties. No shame in that. But glamour wasn't enough for Audrey Hepburn.

She went from country to country. She held dying babies. She got dirt on her face. She didn't change her clothes. And she came back, told us what she'd seen, told us how we might help—and then she went right back out again.

Not long before she died, she went to Somalia, trying to focus world attention on the suffering there. It wasn't glamorous. But I doubt if she ever looked more beautiful.

We'll always have her movies. Remembering her as a fine actress—which she most certainly was—will never be a problem. Her great movie roles are ours forever. But the caring, committed champion for the health and happiness of children—you won't see that role at the video store. And I suspect that, if she had any choice in the matter, it's for that role she'd prefer to be a *role model* for a generation, from now on.

THE LESSONS OF LOY
December 15, 1993

A lot of debate these days about movies and television, but we may need more emphasis on one question: what does entertainment tell our children about the kind of adults we want them to be? Will we respect our sons more if they grow up to be gun-toting Rambos instead of research scientists? Would we prefer our daughters to be bubbleheaded bimbos—instead of research scientists?

At the movies nowadays, you don't see much besides thugs and bimbos. The message at the movies used to be both simpler and wiser. The death last night of movie star Myrna Loy especially reminds me that Hollywood can provide powerful images—role models—of sexiness and beauty, and *brains*.

Myrna Loy could hold her own with any of the big boys: Gable, Tracy, William Powell. Not by trading on her looks or by carrying a gun, but by using her wits.

Loy's most famous role was Nora Charles, the detective's

wife in the *Thin Man* movies. Remember that Nora was a millionaire's daughter, totally out of her element with her husband Nick's friends, gamblers, thieves, and con men. How did she get along? By using her head and her humor. When one of her husband's well-meaning criminal buddies accidentally snatched her purse, Nora only smiled and said, "Oh, Nicky, you do have the *nicest* friends." Tough, smart, and funny.

In real life, Myrna Loy was tough, smart, and funny, too: a committed worker for the American Red Cross and the Democratic party. On the set, she used to raise a fuss whenever no African Americans were hired as extras in crowd scenes. Then, as soon as some African Americans got hired, she'd raise another fuss until the extras had been given briefcases, and had traded their porter's uniforms for business suits. Earlier than most people, Myrna Loy realized that movies tell us a lot about who we are and can be.

That's why her intelligence is so important, whether she's playing a socialite or a gangster's moll. Myrna Loy showed America's daughters (and sons) that brains count in this world, that brains are worth educating, protecting, and showing off.

She wasn't alone. Ginger Rogers, Jean Arthur, and Dale Evans pitched in, too. As did the studios that made the pictures.

But those were the old days. The little girls who grew up watching Myrna Loy are wives and mothers now, teachers, bankers, artists, doctors. Today's little girls may turn out fine—but too many of their Hollywood role models will have been no match for Myrna Loy.

THE LAST GENUINE ARTICLE
August 26, 1998

Jerry Clower made people laugh so hard they cried. And they loved him for it.

The heartland American humorist died August 24 in his native Mississippi.

"I don't tell funny stories," he liked to say. "I tell stories funny."

That's the truth. Jerry Clower's stories could wind on like a country road, and you'd enjoy the scenery so much—the crazy characters and outrageous situations—that you'd quit caring whether you ever got to the punch line.

But the punch lines were good, too.

Perhaps the greatest of all Jerry Clower's stories concerns John Eubanks, "a professional tree climber. He didn't believe in shooting no coon out of no tree. It was against his upbringing."

Clower told how John used to take a crosscut saw whenever he went raccoon hunting. "When you tree a coon," John advised, "hold the dogs and cut the tree down, or either climb the tree and make the coon jump in amongst the dogs. Give him a sporting chance."

Clower remembered: "A lot of times we'd climb a tree and make a coon jump in amongst twenty dogs, but at least he had the option of whipping all them dogs and walking off if he wanted to. This was strictly left up to the coon."

Clower recounted one coon hunting expedition, when he, John Eubanks, and a neighbor, Mr. Barron, treed an animal in "the biggest sweet gum tree in all of the Amite River swamps." Clower dared John to climb up and knock the coon down.

Only it wasn't a coon, it was a lynx. "We called 'em 'souped-up wildcats' in Amite County," Clower would remember.

That thing had great big tusks coming out of his mouth, and great big claws on the end of his feet; and people, that thing attacked John up in the top of that tree.

"Whaw! Ooooo!" You could hear John squalling.

"What's the matter with John?"

"I don't have no idea what in the world's happening to John!"

"Knock him out, John-n-n!"

"WOW! OOOO! This thing's killing me!"

The whole top of the treee was shaking. The dogs got to biting the bark off the tree and fighting one another underneath the tree, and I kicked 'em and said, "You dogs get away!"

"Yow-owooo! This thing's killing me!"

John knew that Mr. Barron toted a pistol in his belt to shoot snakes with. He kept hollering, "Ohhhh, shoot this thing! Have mercy, this thing's killing me! Shoot this thing!"

Mr. Barron said, "John, I can't shoot up in there. I might hit you."

John said, "Well, just shoot up in here amongst us. One of us has got to have some relief!"

There are places where you don't have to tell the whole story (I've abridged it considerably here)—all you have to do is say, "One of us has got to have some *relief*!" and you'll make friends.

If Jerry Clower had never done anything but tell that story, he'd have been a legend.

Clower used to insist that most of his stories really happened. Maybe so, maybe not. They were always *honest*. Clower got his start selling fertilizer, and he quickly learned that audiences can tell the difference between honesty and . . . fertilizer.

Clower grew up in grinding rural poverty in Amite County,

Mississippi. But he was smart, and he wanted an education. After serving in the U.S. Navy, Clower put himself through Mississippi State University playing football.

Working for a chemical company, he learned that a funny story can make a sale. So he worked up an informal routine and wound up the most welcome fertilizer salesman in Mississippi.

Somebody passed a tape of Jerry along to MCA, a fancy recording company with offices in Nashville and Hollywood. They immediately spotted Jerry as a major talent. But the story goes that Jerry didn't want to sign—until they mentioned that, in addition to Elton John, they also handled Ernest Tubb.

Thirty days later, Jerry had his first gold album. He became a fixture on the stage of the Grand Ol' Opry. And a genuine American success story.

Clower stuck to his roots. When he was still poor, he married his childhood sweetheart, Homerline. They stayed married for fifty years, until death parted them.

He preferred bright red or yellow suits. He pronounced his first name "JAY-ree" in an accent so purely Mississippi, it seemed to have its own delta. And his voice rolled like an old coon hound's.

Nowadays, comedians are a dime a dozen. Most are fakes. They use dirty words whenever they can't think of a real joke, which is most of the time.

A devout Baptist, Clower never told a story that couldn't be repeated in your grandmother's presence. Or, as he liked to put it, "I ain't never made an album you can't play in church."

It's hard to find a comedian who's funny to old and young, black and white, city and country folk—but this reporter has never met anybody who heard Clower and didn't like him.

Today scholars study Clower's humor. They compare him to Mark Twain. They say the trouble with that other Mississippian, William Faulkner, was he was too serious and not enough like Jerry Clower.

As Faulkner wrote of Yoknapatawpha County, Clower told of Yazoo City. As Faulkner described the Compson family, so Clower had his vast Ledbetter clan: Uncle Versie, Aunt Pet, and their children, Arnell, Burnell, Raynell, Lanell, W. L., Odell, Udell, Marcel, Claude, Newgene, and Clovis. Odell is famous for having finished in two weeks a puzzle that was marked "4 to 7 Years."

Advanced students know all about the Ledbetters' innumerable aunts, uncles, and cousins, including Miss Flossie, the only college-educated Ledbetter, who insists on visiting a big-city sperm bank and winds up having a baby when she's sixty-five. She can't show the baby to the neighbors, however, because she can't remember where she laid him down.

Clower claimed the Ledbetters were his neighbors, and Marcel his best friend growing up. They joined the Navy together right after high school, Clower said, and were on a train to the base when Marcel tasted his first banana. Just as Marcel began to eat, the train entered a long, dark tunnel.

> *Marcel said, "Whooo! Jerry, Jerry!"*
> *I said, "What?"*
> *He said, "Have you et your banana yet?"*
> *I said, "Nah."*
> *He said, "Well, don't. I took one bite of mine and went stone blind."*

According to Clower, Marcel recently ran for Congress. Marcel denied that he'd been mud-slinging. "I didn't tell them people you were ignorant," Marcel told his opponent. "I don't know how they found it out."

As always, the stories were *honest* even when they weren't precisely *accurate*.

His comedy albums sound better on cassette tapes—eight-track, if you can find 'em—in the cab of a pickup or an eighteen-wheeler late at night.

I am convinced that Clower's stories have done as much for highway safety as seat belts and speed limits in some parts of the country.

As of this writing, the *New York Times* still has not published Clower's obituary. City slickers. What do they know?

In truck stops and trailer parks, on front porches and in feed stores, they're hanging their heads. Jerry Clower is gone. He was the genuine article. Maybe the last.

MANTLE
August 14, 1995

Years ago, when he was just a teenager at Commerce High School, they called him the "Commerce Comet." But that was when he ran the bases on a dry patch of land in Oklahoma, not far from the zinc mines where his father worked. The Comet went on to soar far beyond the prairies of Oklahoma, blazing a place in history. And now the light has dimmed. Mickey Mantle has died.

He will be eulogized and mourned. Tributes will be written. Speeches will be made. Flags will be lowered over countless sparse green playing fields, and young men will take off their caps and bow their heads, and throughout the bleachers there will echo a terrible silence. Mickey Mantle, "The Mick," is gone.

He lived just sixty-three years—but what years they were. The facts will be repeated again and again. How he holds the all-time World Series home-run record. How he hit the longest home run ever—565 feet. How he won baseball's triple crown back in 1956. How he battled bad knees, and alcoholism, and finally the disease that claimed him, cancer.

But more than the facts of that extraordinary life, this magnificent Yankee embodied something unique. At a particular moment in the American Century, he represented all that America was and could be.

An America of great strides and powerful swings, able to hit the ball out of the park. An America of heroes hoisted on shoulders, and ticker tape parades, and men who achieve greatness with cleats on their feet and a bat in their hands. An America where sportsmanship came first and business second.

Mickey Mantle was part of all that, and more. How much more, we didn't realize until the end. In his last months, he faced his greatest challenge like a champion, with grace and courage.

Baseball is a game measured by runs, hits, and errors. Mantle would have been the first to admit that in baseball, and in life, he had a fair amount of all those.

But, as every fan knows, a baseball player has just one goal.

It is a goal Mickey Mantle achieved hundreds of times on the ball field. And on a summer morning, this boy of summer did it one last time.

Mickey Mantle made it home.

CBS News writer Greg Kandra wrote the preceding essay for radio broadcast on Dan Rather Reporting.

ALONE
June 19, 1996

In Moscow this weekend to cover the Russian elections, my assistant and I were caught by a voice in the darkness.

It was about three in the morning, and already we could see

the early dawn of Russian summer. We had just filed our last report, and were trudging back to the hotel for a few hours' sleep.

Then we heard the voice. There wasn't a star in the Moscow sky, but she was singing about moonlight in Vermont. You had to stand still. It was as if the voice were a hand, holding you in place.

The voice was Ella Fitzgerald's. The American singer died over the weekend. Already obituary writers were trying to find words to describe her, pulling up old quotes ("Poor Ella can't play piano, all she can do is sing perfectly")—all weekend, even in Moscow, we heard every tired line.

Frank Rich, a critic and columnist in the *New York Times*, complained about all the attention given to Ella Fitzgerald's *perfection*, her undeniably astonishing ability to hit notes and project lyrics with flawless technique, as if she were simply a musical instrument. People have been comparing Ella to Billie Holiday. True, Ella was more restrained, never a tragedienne like Billie Holiday. But, Frank Rich asked, if Ella was only technically perfect, how come her songs are so moving? She must have felt *something*, said Rich, although he couldn't identify the feeling.

We can. Ella might be singing a happy song or a sad, funny, or despairing one. She might be singing with Louis Armstrong's trumpet, or Duke Ellington's band, or Joe Pass's guitar. But she was always alone.

You heard it in every brilliant note. We heard it in the Moscow night, far from home, far from the America that was always her subject matter. She was alone the way we were alone.

Hearing is the lonely sense, the sense that sneaks up on us, that creeps through the ears and into the soul. With her voice, Ella Fitzgerald could make you listen, and believe, and remember. She could enter the dark quiet rooms inside your head, slip right in and never leave. Because she was always alone—singing—for you alone.

We never knew much about her personal life. We never

really knew anything about her except what she told us in her songs, quietly, for us alone to know. Maybe we're not supposed to be able to describe such things. Maybe that's what songs are for—for the things you can't say with words alone.

THE HEROISM OF MARRIED LOVE
February 10, 1999

We have been passing around a little book, my wife, Jean, and I and a few friends. It is hardly any bigger than a book of Green Stamps, but we keep picking it up and passing it along, returning to it and discussing it among ourselves.

It is called *Elegy for Iris* (St. Martin's Press, 1999), and it is about married love.

It is also about Alzheimer's, and growing old, and remembering and forgetting, and finding peace.

It is about Iris Murdoch, the English novelist and philosopher who died this week; her husband, John Bayley, a critic, novelist, and teacher, wrote the book.

But it is mainly about marriage.

The book already broke our hearts and mended them before Iris Murdoch died.

I confess that I once picked up a novel by Iris Murdoch. I read several chapters before I decided the book was not—could not—be written in English. Michael Jordan couldn't have written anything further over my head. I never read John Bayley's work at all, until now.

The occasional foray into Cormac McCarthy aside, the nearest I usually come to a philosophical novel on the nature of good and evil (Ms. Murdoch's specialty) is when Jean tries to foist Marcel Proust on me with the ingenuous recommendation that "it's just as good as Dan Jenkins, really."

Elegy for Iris has seduced me, with its painstaking reconstruction of the love between two people. From their earliest days as self-conscious Oxford intellectuals, Iris and John surprised each other—and themselves—with the depth of their feelings. They found love easier than marriage, but they went on surprising for forty-five years.

Several years ago Murdoch complained of writer's block; then a doctor diagnosed her with Alzheimer's. By the time Bayley began to write his *Elegy* she had slipped deep into the disease.

She was one of the smartest women in Britain, and one of the most acclaimed authors of the century. She was fiercely independent, often taking great pains to prevent friends and lovers from knowing about each other, to say nothing of permitting them to know each other.

With Alzheimer's, that famous intelligence was dragged down by a memory that could no longer function. That flourishing gift for language withered, until she couldn't complete a spoken sentence. That fierce independence was subdued, until she relied entirely on her husband.

Readers will find that Alzheimer's could destroy almost everything except the love between John and Iris. And in his book, John set about safeguarding that love—the times and books, ideas, and adventures they'd shared—by remembering, because Iris no longer could.

John knew that their love had always been the most important part of their lives. It still was. And, I daresay, it still is.

There's not a married person on earth who doesn't fear the lingering illness of a spouse. Life doesn't offer many tests of character more difficult than that, and most of us fear that we won't be strong enough for ourselves, much less strong enough for *both* of us.

John Bayley was strong enough. And so was Iris Murdoch.

I want to share that. I want to report to you that there is, right now at your library or bookstore, a book whose main characters are heroic just because they are married to each other.

In another husband's memoir, I find my mother and father, my wife's parents, our friends, and us. I find shared lives, and hurts and forgivenesses, and joys that are the greatest because nobody else knows them.

Happy Valentine's Day. Pass it on.

Iris Murdoch died monday, February 8, 1999.

LOVE ME TENDER
August 15, 1997

Some years ago, when my wife, Jean, was a girl in Winchester, Texas, a young man came through town. He was a truck driver, good-looking kid, with hair like the raven's wing and deep, deep eyes that looked right at her and seemed to say, *How do you do, ma'am, would you like to dance?*

Since she happened to be *at* a dance, Jeannie answered, "Yes."

And ever since that dance, at the V.F.W. post in Winchester, Texas, on a warm summer night many, many years ago, Jeannie has been . . .

. . . an Elvis Presley fan.

For the handsome young fellow who danced with her that night was *not* this reporter, but Elvis Aron Presley himself. A few months later, he gave up truck-driving for a career in music. Later, my wife met me. The rest is history.

I can never forget that, if things had worked out differently, Jean might have been Mrs. Presley, Elvis might have anchored at CBS News, and I still wouldn't be able to carry a tune in a bucket.

Elvis Presley died twenty years ago this week.

He left behind a lot of fans. Elvis sang and strummed about hopes and fears familiar to everyone. Love looked for, love found, love lost. Smiles and sorrows, raunchiness and reserve, spirituality. These were his core, his DNA of feelings and thoughts.

As a performer, Elvis's instincts were more powerful than anybody else's training. He had a lot of *hey, look at me* in him, but once you did look, he followed through with plenty to listen to. His music brought together many styles, just as it continues to bring together many audiences. His appeal crossed every barrier, and would forever change the standards of contemporary culture.

As a performer, he was bold, but in private he was self-effacing. The spontaneity that propelled him to be so dynamic onstage seemed to cause him just as quickly to withdraw into himself. He was just as needy as anyone else, his friends realized, but he could step outside himself, answer the muse of individual expression, and tug at our heartstrings.

In Southern parts, they call it "Saturday night and Sunday morning." Sure, you can raise the roof, but you'll have to atone for it the next day. So the voice that could sing "Jail House Rock" could turn around and sing "Oh How I Love Jesus."

Why do we still miss Elvis, twenty years later? Because he sang songs to help us live life, to make us appreciate the good times and carry on in the tough times.

He made it a little easier for me to turn to my Jeannie and say, "Love me tender."

Chapter 5

THE LIGHTER SIDE

I DON'T WANT MY MTV,
OR BRING BACK THE TEST PATTERN!
October 29, 1997

On the highway these days, you can't help noticing the familiar flicker of the television set shining in the windows—of other vehicles. Not just luxury limousines: some buses now have rows of little TV sets suspended over the seats.

Passengers can now enjoy the earthbound equivalent of an in-flight movie. Some bus lines even feature broadcast TV, so you won't miss the big game just because you had to visit Aunt Martha. They'd offer cable if they could make the cords long enough. Satellite dishes must be next.

This might endanger drivers of other vehicles, especially if there's a really good basketball game, and the highway's dark and the screens are bright, and if you pull up a little, you could get a better view of Michael Jordan making that shot. . . .

However, for reasons apart from traffic safety, this trend of TV in buses disturbs your reporter.

It means there's almost *no* place left in this country where you can go without being entertained.

Americans today demand entertainment. We expect it. We're surprised when there's not entertainment everywhere. We punish those who dare to be dull.

How did entertainment become ubiquitous? Some blame *Sesame Street,* which showed that learning could be entertaining.

When I was a boy, learning wasn't entertaining. It was hard work. We didn't have "New Math." We had *old* math. The kind that made your brain sweat. The kind you dreaded.

But you remembered it.

When I got my first job in broadcasting, even TV didn't always entertain: sometimes it informed, enlightened, uplifted.

Reporters didn't entertain. They reported.

Politicians didn't entertain (not intentionally). On the floor of the legislature, they looked like mummies. None of this playacting on C-SPAN you see today. (Some of them *did* know how to give a good stump speech: they'd talk the hounds out from under the porch.)

We didn't have television sets on buses, or in many homes. Now they're even putting TV sets in public bathrooms. (Why should anybody miss a minute of *General Hospital*?)

Mostly, if we wanted entertainment, we went to the movies—or read a book. We had radio, but radio kept your hands and feet (and mind) free to work.

Well, I'm not hanging back with the fogeys. I'm embracing progress (if that's what it is). I'm gonna be "fly."

(Actually, I was content to be "hep," or even "with it," but it's not allowed anymore.)

Anyway, I have a few suggestions. Because it turns out there are a few places in this country still awaiting entertainment—at least a TV set in the corner.

Operating Rooms. Sure, they call it an operating "theater," but it's not really entertaining. Ask anybody who's had major surgery.

Restaurants. Why should the fact that you're eating out mean that you look at your dinner companions any more than you do when you're eating in front of the television at home?

The Stock Exchange. You think the folks on the trading floor don't need a little *Touched by an Angel* these days?

The Voting Booth. Pitifully few Americans vote. They say elections are about nothing. So is *Seinfeld.* Put 'em together, and maybe voter turnouts will improve.

The Ballet. Star Trek Voyager consistently outperforms *Swan Lake* in the Nielsens. Sorry.

The Womb and the Tomb. Most advertisers consider the unborn and the unbreathing to be unattractive demographic groups. But they are captive audiences, and what else are they supposed to do with all that free time?

The World Series. Think how exciting it would've been if fans in the stands could've channel-surfed during this year's match, the Marlins versus the Indians versus *The Simpsons.*

THE DUMB BASS
August 27, 1997

AUSTIN, TEXAS—In my experience, the folks most likely to talk about the "wily" bass, the "elusive" perch, or the "cunning" trout are the folks most likely to have a crease in their waders and starch in their nets.

They're the ones who spend more money on equipment than they spend time coaxing the fish out of the water. "Status fishers," I call them, or "pond yuppies" or "brook brothers." Serious fishers, which is what I aspire to be, don't pay these people much attention except when they're scaring the fish.

The great challenge of catching a fish doesn't have much to do with brains—fish brains. All fish are created pretty much equal, and pretty much dumb.

Or so I'd always thought, until I talked with Dick Luebke of the Heart of the Hills Research Station in Ingram, Texas. "I don't ever frame it in terms of intelligence," says Mr. Luebke. "All I say is that some fish are more catchable than others."

Inspired by the increasing popularity of catch-and-release fishing over the past decade or so, he and his colleagues with the Texas Parks and Wildlife Department tried to breed fish for catchability.

They started with some bass, both the Florida bass and the northern or largemouth variety. They tried to catch these bass and learned that, in any given location, 30 percent of the fish weren't catchable. But the biologists marked all the fish they caught, and then tossed them back. And they marked them again every time they caught them again. Finally, they separated all the bass that had been caught several times from all the bass that hadn't been caught at all. The catchable bass were then encouraged to make little catchable bass, and so on.

"The study took four years," says Mr. Luebke. "I thought we needed about three generations to confirm our observations." By the time they'd developed whole schools of stupid fish (you might call them "remedial schools"), they were ready to make it official: "there is a genetic factor to the catchability trait."

This is by no means a frivolous inquiry. Fishing can mean big business in tourism and equipment sales. "Where the fish bite, the dollars flow," says Mr. Luebke, quickly adding, "and the enjoyment, too." He estimates that anglers spend $30 million every year at one typical Texas lake alone. A fishing area is more likely to catch on, he says, if it gets a reputation for good catch rates of desirable fish, such as bass.

"Nothing turns people on to fishing faster than catching fish," says Mr. Luebke, "and nothing turns them off surer than standing for hours and not catching anything."

Well, I generally admire the efforts of the Texas Parks and Wildlife Department, who take special care of everything from picnic tables and campgrounds to bluebonnets and endangered species. But I'm a little worried about the results of this particular experiment.

With microwave ovens, condensed books, digital watches, and Velcro shoelaces, haven't we made life easy enough yet? What will become of our national character when fish are bred so dumb that they jump out of the water and into the frying pan?

And how will Texans respond when they learn the most shocking result of all?

Mr. Luebke and his colleagues found that the Florida bass

were much more difficult to catch than the largemouth bass. The largemouth is the species native to Texas.

In other words, it's true what some people have been trying all along to tell this reporter, who is a largemouth Texas native himself: there's no dumb bass like a Texan dumb bass.

IT'S BEGINNING TO LOOK
A LOT LIKE EASTER
November 26, 1997

Is Thanksgiving over yet? It's been going on so long, I can't tell.

It used to be that the holidays respected *seasons*. Not anymore. Halloween decorations went up just before Labor Day.

It used to be, I could get pretty excited about Halloween. It's a children's holiday, full of fun and candy. How is anybody, much less anybody with the attention span of the average American five-year-old, supposed to maintain any enthusiasm for Halloween over a period of more than two months?

They say this has something to do with commercialism, that Halloween is now the second-biggest marketing season—after Christmas. But how much candy can you eat, and how long can it take to pick a costume? I mean, really: two *months*? I've seen wars planned and executed in less time.

As for Christmas—I am now so confused, I can't tell whether I'm supposed to be shopping for *this* Christmas, or *next* Christmas, or *last* Christmas, or Easter. It's all blending together.

In New York, it's beginning to look a lot like Christmas—year-round. Santa Claus opened the Christmas show at Radio City Music Hall almost a month ago. And Christmas, Hanukkah, and Kwanzaa decorations have been up in stores for weeks, crowding out all the Pilgrims and pumpkins that had been in stores since . . . August.

This is happening all over the country, not just in New York City.

If they thought they could make a dollar on it, July Fourth sales would start in March.

I used to look forward to holidays. Now I don't know how to look forward to holidays. I can't see that far into the future.

Nothing respects seasons anymore—not merchandisers, not holidays, not anything or anybody.

It used to be that, if you turned on the television and saw somebody playing a particular sport, you knew what time of year it was. (This was especially handy if you'd been in a coma.) Football in autumn, basketball in winter, and baseball in spring or summer.

Now football season starts in July, baseball shivers as much as it sweats, and basketball season never really stops—immediately after play-offs and championships, summer leagues start, flowing into preseason exhibitions.

It used to be politicians started running for President in the summer of an election year. Guess what? The race for 2000 has been going on for more than a year. Pundits are already declaring front-runners.

It used to be you could only get tomatoes and peaches in summer, oranges in winter. Squash used to be divided into categories: winter and summer. For a reason. If you wanted a butternut squash, you had to wait until the weather got cold.

Forgive me, but food *tasted* better when you had to wait for it. No matter when you were ready. You ate food when it was ready (the word we used was "ripe").

Nowadays people laugh when I tell them that tomatoes used to taste like tomatoes. My journalistic credibility is at risk.

Even in Houston, where I grew up, the seasons were respected. This in a town where the four seasons are known as: summer, almost-summer, late-summer, and not-summer.

It used to be that you never ate watermelon in Texas until after Juneteenth. That's the day, June 19, 1865, when most slaves in Texas and Louisiana were finally told they'd been freed. The legend grew up that watermelon eaten after Juneteenth would taste sweeter, and throughout Texas people of every color and creed abided by that custom.

And you know what? The watermelon *did* taste sweeter.

Nowadays you can have watermelon for Thanksgiving. If you can remember when Thanksgiving is.

DON'T LET IT BE FORGOT FOR
ONE BRIEF SHINING MOMENT
December 10, 1997

This reporter was shocked, *shocked* to discover—in a stunning book—that Camelot had a dark side.

I'm not talking about Seymour Hersh's new book about the Kennedys. I'm talking about Sir Thomas Malory's old book, *Le Morte d'Arthur*. Because it turns out the dark side of Camelot was there in plain sight, all along.

For your convenience, I've itemized the allegations:

Collaboration with a Foreign Dictatorship. The historical King Arthur (if one existed) may have been an imperial commander left behind after Rome's retreat from Britain. But other scholars suggest a foreign political influence even more alarming: by most accounts, Arthur spoke nothing but *French.*

Witchcraft. Although Arthur styled himself a devout Roman Catholic, his principal adviser practiced magic arts, and Arthur credited most of his early successes to Merlin's enchantments. Knights of the Round Table regularly encountered dozens of sorcerers, witches, potions, curses, and spells. Even Arthur's sword, Excalibur, was gotten by supernatural means.

Embezzlement. Neither Excalibur nor any part of Arthur's armor, mostly purchased with public funds, has ever been retrieved. Experts estimate that a single cuirass or halberd could fetch six figures at auction.

Secret Early Marriage. Sure, we remember his *second* wife—but was there really a first? Scholars now say there wasn't—only because King Arthur's youthful liaison with Morgause was never legitimized. Lucky thing, too: she was his sister. Their child, Mordred, would later overthrow Camelot and assassinate Arthur.

Conspiracy. But did Mordred act alone? At the very least, he received help from his mother. Later, Arthur's body was taken to the Lady of the Lake and escorted to Avalon in a barge steered by three veiled ladies—none of whom were ever seen again. Doubts about Arthur's assassination grew up almost immediately: to this day, some Britons believe that Arthur didn't die at all. They say his body has been preserved at Avalon, and that he will return some day to rule England again.

Adultery. Most of Arthur's knights spent more time bedding goodwives than rescuing maidens. Chief on the list: Lancelot, whose dalliance with Queen Guinevere brought Camelot to its knees; and Tristan, whose affair with Isolde, wife of King Mark, still causes tongues to wag (albeit mostly at the opera house).

Miscellaneous Womanizing. Lancelot also slept with Elaine, the Lily Maid of Astolat, a one-night stand that produced Sir Galahad. Merlin the Enchanter was seduced and imprisoned by Vivien (a.k.a. Nimue), a nymph several hundred years his junior. And most knights had their amorous adventures recorded in long poems called "lays." (I can't go into more detail in a family newspaper.)

Abuse of Power. Despite their credo that "Might Isn't Right," the Knights of the Round Table were extremely violent and well armed; they practiced numerous tortures in addition to murders and executions, often on the flimsiest of pretenses (see the case of Sir Gawain versus the Green Knight). Despite rampant poverty and other domestic woes, Arthur depleted the English treasuries by questing for the Holy Grail over a period of some twenty years. Historians never conclusively determined that the Grail ever existed.

Credibility Gap. For that matter, historians have never conclusively determined that Arthur, the Round Table, Camelot, or any of the rest existed. Most of the legends we now repeat grew up in medieval times, the subject of minstrels and troubadours, in a tradition of courtly romance established by Queen Eleanor of Aquitaine (another English royal whose private life would raise eyebrows, then as now).

Given today's standards, Arthur's image would be so tarnished that many scholars doubt he'd be able to rule. But some still wonder if Camelot's legend could endure without its "dark side."

IT TAKES TWO . . . AND A CONSIDERABLE AMOUNT OF CHUTZPAH
October 16, 1997

Item: Dateline, Buenos Aires, Argentina—President Bill Clinton and First Lady Hillary Rodham Clinton have been intrigued by the tango.

Not so intrigued that they have actually danced it. Not yet, anyway. Not so far as anyone knows.

While on their current series of Latin American visits, they have been entertained by various exhibitions of the sultry South American dance. This has included a stop at a nightspot named Señor Tango.

The First Couple, it is reported, ate a steak and watched the tango.

What they said to each other inside this (apparently) Argentine version of a combined steakhouse and honky-tonk has not been reported.

But your narrator is willing to bet that sometime, at least one time, somewhere along about the shank of the evening, Hillary whispered to Bill, "Let's try it." Or, at the very least, "Honey, why can't *we* do that?"

This belief is based on personal experience. It's what the First Lady of the Rather House has said to *her* husband in similar circumstances over the years.

You know, you're just sitting there, maybe downing a few sarsaparillas after dining on good steak, you're watching some Arthur Murray School graduates gliding around or tearing up the linoleum with some complicated dance. Mama gets enthralled and wants to get up and give it a go. The old man ain't about to. Too afraid of making a stumbling, bumbling fool of himself.

The Charleston, the bop, the Chicken, the samba, the lambada, the macarena. Whatever.

Yessir, and no ma'am. Here is one man who can sympathize with the President in his response of: "No tango, no way, and, waiter, may I please have another two fingers of that sarsaparilla?"

Mind you, dear listener, this is written and broadcast by one who has never been known as what you might call smooth on the dance floor.

The Texas Two-step and the old San Jacinto Junior College Shuffle are about all this man could ever muster, and neither of them very well. (Well, maybe, on some nights, under just the right conditions sometime long after midnight at just the right, *real* honky-tonk, *maybe* I could muster a sorry version of a jitterbug. But that's it.)

So, however one may feel about Bill Clinton, President,

many of us can definitely identify with him as Bill Clinton, Wallflower.

The tango is beautiful, wonderful, sultry, seductive, romantic, and all that. But *not* something a man wants to do when the whole world is watching.

WHEN SCANDAL ROCKS
THE WHITE HOUSE
January 28, 1998

Reimagining Abraham Lincoln's preparation for the Gettysburg Address is a time-honored formula for writers as diverse as Eric Sevareid and Bob Newhart. The events of a furious few days in January 1998 had me wondering: how would Honest Abe hold up under today's brand of blistering scrutiny of presidential private lives?

"Mr. President, sir, we need to talk to you about certain allegations . . . about your past."

"What on earth are you talking about?"

"Joshua Fry Speed, sir. The man you boarded with for nearly four years while you were young bachelors in Springfield. He's come forward now to say that you shared a bed during all that time."

"Now, hold on a minute. You don't actually think—"

"Sir, it doesn't matter what I think: this could cost you in your reelection campaign. You could lose the South."

"I'm at *war* with the South, you idiot. Besides, I have nothing to be ashamed about."

"You don't really expect people to believe that, do you? There goes our whole 'Honest' image."

"There's nothing sexual about this."

"Is, sir? Is? Present tense?"

"Past, future, infinitive: nothing! Times were tough, beds were few, and we made adjustments. People do such things all the time."

"People aren't politicians, sir."

"I don't have time for this. I have to get ready for my speech in Pennsylvania tomorrow."

"Sir, your attorneys think it's highly inadvisable for you to make any public statement at this time. There could be repercussions, perhaps indictments."

"Nonsense! Our brave men, living and dead, have given the last full measure of their devotion, that this nation might live."

"Yeah, yeah, yeah. Frankly, sir, if you insist on making the speech, you'll have to delete any reference to 'men.' Under the circumstances, there might be snickers."

"Under *what* circumstances? I have no circumstances! I have a speech to give. How am I supposed to dedicate a military cemetery without mentioning men?"

"Unfortunately, sir, a lot of people have doubts about the strength of your marriage as it stands. There are rumors that Mrs. Lincoln beats you, that she's an opium addict and a Southern spy."

"She'd be a poor spy if she were an opium addict, wouldn't she?"

"She still uses her maiden name: Mary Todd Lincoln. Sends the wrong message, sir."

"Oh, brother. Look over my speech notes if you like."

"Envelope, huh? Nice touch. Oh, this is all wrong: 'Fourscore and seven years ago, our fathers—' Where are the mothers? Where are the babes?"

"I haven't got time for this. I have to explain to the country that government of the people, by the people, for the people must not perish from the earth."

"Sir, I don't know how to get through to you. There will be newspaper reporters present—telegraph operators—whatever you say could make headlines within *days*! This is a crisis. The American people won't stand two sexually ambiguous Presidents in succession."

"You mean James Buchanan—?"

"I'm afraid so, sir. You see how much is at stake. We're thinking it might help to get a dog, split a few rails, play with your children—you know, show the people that you're a regular guy."

"In the middle of my speech?"

"Don't take it so seriously, sir. It's only one speech. And you're really irrelevant to the whole process. I mean, in a larger sense, you cannot dedicate, you cannot consecrate, you cannot hallow that ground. The brave soldiers who struggled there have consecrated it far above your poor power to add or detract."

"I'm still not sure."

"Leave everything to us, sir. If you're lucky, the world will little note, nor long remember, what you say at Gettysburg."

CARTOON CARNIVAL
November 25, 1992

Years ago, the government tried to tell us that ketchup was a vegetable. At least, ketchup qualified as a vegetable in school lunch programs. Not at embassy dinners. Just at lunch tables for America's kids.

Years ago, a certain amount of television time had to be allotted to public affairs programming. But those requirements bit the dust. One result: you don't see as many documentaries on television as you used to. (Maybe you'd be watching something else if they were there, but they're not there.) A few requirements remain in place for television. One of them is that a certain amount of programming time has to go to educational broadcasts. Consider those the vegetables on the television menu.

Now the networks are trying to tell you that the Saturday morning cartoon shows are not only entertaining, but educational.

According to the networks, many shows teach kids important values and social skills, such as cooperation, teamwork, and community. And action heroes teach kids the benefits of sports and exercise, presumably because they have so many muscles and can protect themselves against bad guys.

And all those fuzzy little animal shows must teach kids . . . well, I'm still trying to figure that one out.

We were in the mood for some educational television the other day, so we turned on *The Bugs Bunny & Tweety Show*. That's on ABC. We wanted to be objective by watching another network's show. And the cartoons on *Bugs Bunny & Tweety* are old Warner Brothers cartoons, acknowledged classics. If the Saturday morning cartoon shows are educational, then *Bugs Bunny & Tweety* must be the equivalent of *Moby-Dick* or *The Scarlet Letter*.

So what did we learn?

1. Rabbits can talk. So can cats, birds, and skunks. Lions cannot talk. Neither can bears. Some dogs can talk; most don't. Coyotes and roadrunners communicate mostly through sign boards (in English or Latin), which they cleverly conceal about them until needed.
2. French people are sex-obsessed. Italian people eat constantly. German people are fat.
3. It is okay to hit people over the head, shoot them full of lead, push them over cliffs, crush them under boulders, feed them sticks of dynamite . . . because they will spring

back to normal, without a scratch, in a matter of seconds.

We were willing to accept that not all children's cartoon shows were just excuses to sell toys and lunch boxes. Some of them are fun. Some of them really are classics.

But educational? For children?

Is anybody learning anything from this episode?

CONSCIOUSNESS SCHOOL
July 29, 1993

Today more proof, if any were necessary, that California is not like other places.

We've received some course descriptions from John F. Kennedy University out there in San Francisco, evidently a perfectly normal university with a Law School and a School of Management and . . . a "Graduate School for the Study of Human Consciousness."

Let that sink in a moment. Human consciousness is something that many college students I've known did their best to avoid. Here, they want you to *study* consciousness, and presumably you have to be conscious to study it.

What do they mean by this "Human Consciousness"? According to a university publication, "The school offers master's degree programs that explore the various facets of human experience: education, communication, psychology and counseling, art and creativity, movement, research, leadership. Examination and application of spiritual principles are the threads which weave these programs together and distinguish them from other graduate programs."

That's not so bad. So why give the school such an odd name? Why not call it The School of Art-and-Psychology-and-Philosophy, so that people from the East Coast and Midwest could feel more comfortable?

Course offerings include:

Theory and Practice of Dreams. "Honestly, Professor Wagstaff, I wasn't sleeping in class—I was only practicing my dreams. And I was just getting the hang of it when you woke me up."

Topics in Art and Consciousness: Art and Wholeness. "Dear Professor Corey, I couldn't hand in my project today because I wasn't feeling whole. Only partial."

Global Issues. Also known as "Things and Stuff."

Methods of Self-exploration. The lab for this one must be a doozy.

The Nature of Reality. Interested students may opt for the second semester: "The Reality of Nature."

No kidding, there's a course on writing research term papers with an instructor whose last name is Delay.

There's another course on "Conscious Careers in the Nineties." In the eighties, we were all supposed to be too career-conscious. Now we're supposed to have conscious careers. Please note the subtle but important distinction.

But be warned: another university publication says that "graduates of these programs are creating new career paths." Translation: this degree may not help you get a job in a tough economy.

Well, we wish these people luck, and we hope they're learning a lot (something to teach those of us who don't live in California), even if we don't quite understand.

Which makes me think about setting up a Graduate School for Not Quite Understanding. Might do pretty well.

IF A COMPLEX SERIES OF BIOLOGICAL
RESPONSES BE THE FOOD OF LOVE...
February 12, 1993

Maybe you saw the *Time* magazine cover story examining the scientific explanations for love. There's at least one bit of good news. It turns out that love probably isn't a cultural phenomenon, an invention of Western European artists and nobles, as historians had been telling us for several years. Love may not make the world go 'round, but at least it gets 'round the world: anthropologists find evidence of it just about everywhere, including places that never saw a production of *Romeo and Juliet*.

But say you feel a Tender Pash, say your life is one big Gershwin song—say you're in love. Who or what's to blame?

The prime suspect seems to be neurochemistry. Love, many scientists now say, is a complex biological process that is even less romantic than breeding instincts or genetic imperatives or cultural tradition. You could almost process love in a test tube, if you were so inclined. Rocks could do it.

Happy Valentine's Day.

And, by the way, *Time* magazine quoted one scientist who called those chemicals "narcotic." Might as well face it. You're addicted to love.

This is about as romantic as a periodic table of the elements. Makes you wonder why you should bother—if you've even got a choice.

Well, your reporter didn't go to school just to eat his lunch. Or to take chemistry labs, as it happens. But I do remember a thing or two about history.

Consider that in mid-February we observe not only the Feast of St. Valentine, but also the birthday of America's sixteenth President, Abraham Lincoln. If looks determined professions, he'd have wound up a circus geek. Serious as a tax audit. Always had his mind on something else. They say he had his charms—nice manners and compelling eyes—well, you can see the eyes for yourself in pictures. But this was not heart-throb material.

He fell in love twice. Once with a girl who died. Then, with pretty, fun-loving Mary Todd. Abraham Lincoln married her. It wasn't an easy marriage. Children died. Enemies accused Mary of being a Southern spy. She was high-strung, difficult, possibly insane.

In the meantime, gawky Abe Lincoln, backwoods lawyer, was one of the greatest leaders, and perhaps *the* greatest President, this country ever had. He possessed a great mind, a tender heart, and a mighty soul. He saved this country. And he loved his wife.

Chemicals? Instinct? We should all be so lucky.

Quite frankly, if love was good enough for Abraham Lincoln, it's good enough for me.

THAT'S ENTERTAINMENT?
March 17, 1999

It's time for the Academy Awards ceremony again, which means it's time for this reporter to realize how few movies he gets to see in the course of a year.

All kinds of movies are nominated that I barely knew existed, or really wanted to see but never got to. Not to mention smash hits I thought I saw, when it turns out I only saw the trailer or the newspaper ad, and really I'm thinking of some other picture entirely.

Last year was especially confusing because many of the movies looked and sounded alike. Doesn't it ever occur to the studios to compare notes? Like, "Hey, we're already making that movie, go make something else"?

Consider the following:

- Joseph Fiennes, Geoffrey Rush, and one of the most talked-about new actresses of our time star in this surprisingly popular costume drama set in the sexy sixteenth century. Is it *Elizabeth* or *Shakespeare in Love*?
- A fabled American director takes a searing look at World War II. Is it *Saving Private Ryan* or *The Thin Red Line*?
- Sex, drugs, and thumpa-thumpa music collide in a legendary nightclub. Is it *54* or *The Last Days of Disco*?
- Politics makes strange bedfellows. Is it *Bullworth* or *Primary Colors*?
- Talking bugs fight to save their colony from hostile forces. Is it *Antz* or *A Bug's Life*?
- Christina Ricci stars as a potty-mouthed teen in this quirky independent feature. Is it—oh, come on. Don't *all* quirky independent features star Christina Ricci as a potty-mouthed teen?
- Planet Earth is threatened by a disaster of intergalactic proportions. Is it *Armageddon, Deep Impact* . . . or *The Avengers*?

Mind you, *one* motion picture costs more than the gross national product of many small nations.

In this era of cost-cutting and corporate mergers, it's a waste of money to produce *two* films on the same subject in the same year, just as it's a waste of my time to see them both. (It's also a waste of theater owners' resources. After all, the local multiplex only has twenty-four screens.)

I've been wondering: if Fernanda Montenegro in *Central Station* were portrayed by Meryl Streep *faking* a Brazilian accent, don't you think she'd win the Best Actress statuette?

But more to the point, wouldn't it be easier if Hollywood

just merged its competing productions? Or if theater owners played two movies at once?

I've been working on treatments for a few screenplays:

- *Saving Meg Ryan.* While on a dangerous mission to rescue a missing soldier behind enemy lines, Tom Hanks carries on a flirtatious correspondence . . . never realizing that the missing soldier is really his secret love.
- *A Bug's Life Is Beautiful (La Vita dell'Insetto è Bella).* A *really* animated father tries to shield his son from the horrors of war with the grasshoppers.
- *Babe: Pig in the City of Angels.* Everybody's favorite talking pig finds true love with Nicolas Cage.
- *Elizabethan Impact.* In the year 1596, Planet Earth is menaced by a giant asteroid. What will Queen Elizabeth (Emma Thompson) do?
- *Elizabethantz.* In the year 1588, an ant colony defends itself from the Spanish Armada.
- *There's Something About Mary, Queen of Scots.* In the year 1587, Ben Stiller realizes there's only one woman he ever truly loved. As the doomed monarch, Cameron Diaz finally gets the Oscar attention she deserves. A hilarious highlight is the beheading sequence, in which part of Stiller's anatomy winds up on the chopping block (I can't go into further detail in family newspapers).

I could go on: *Mulantz* or *The Trumantz Show* just for starters. But I don't have time. I've gotta get to the multiplex to see *Star Wars Episode VII: There's Something About Anakin.*

This column is dedicated to the memory of Gene Siskel (January 26, 1946–February 20, 1999).

ARE WE HAVING FUN YET?
March 29, 1995

Recently, the *Los Angeles Times* reported on the latest conference on "The Healing Power of Laughter and Play," where it was announced that fun is important to health.

Fun alleviates stress, we're told, it can even affect our body chemistry and our immune systems. The experts at the conference prescribe laughter in megadoses.

The *Times* offers a list of ways you and I can have fun. Trouble is that one person's idea of fun—well, look at these examples.

Practice having fun. The *Times* says fun gets easier the more you do it. Suddenly fun is like piano lessons?

Make this your motto: "Things matter, but don't be so serious." The very idea of a motto is antithetical to fun. The nearest thing to a fun motto is "If I could walk that way, I wouldn't need to see a doctor."

Simplify your life. And when you're done with that, I've got some straw you can spin into gold.

Remember that death is part of life. Is this the fun part?

Share your troubles with others; it may open up a way to laugh about it. Or it may simply open up a way for them to laugh about you.

Learn to play a musical instrument. There are those piano lessons again.

Tell funny stories. Fine. But the *Times* actually began this article by pointing out that 96 percent of people can't tell jokes—which is why they provided this list in the first place.

Keep a scrapbook at home of funny things your children say; get out the book and laugh at the memories. That's a pretty good idea. But the *Times* continues by advising us to . . .

Wear a rubber clown nose while scolding your children. Oh, yeah. You can bet your children will have a *ton* of funny remarks for the scrapbook after *that*. They'll be laughing for years to come. So will their psychotherapists.

Take minibreaks throughout the day, about one every ninety minutes, and look for something to laugh about. Take enough such breaks, and you'll need to look for a new job.

At work, bring kazoos to meetings and allow everyone to hum their appreciation of a good idea. Did somebody hum for *this* idea? And what do you do for a *bad* idea?

Hold a "thanks in advance" party for each new employee on the first day of work. At which time you can distribute those handy kazoos.

The list goes on, if you can stand it. I couldn't. My sympathies are all with the reporter who prepared this article. She's got a valuable message, somewhere in there, and a tough job. Telling somebody else how to have fun is *no* fun.

Here's hoping we're all having fun—in our own way. After all, it's seriously important.

COMING TO A THEATER NEAR YOU
September 15, 1995

LOS ANGELES—In this city, the big news is always the movie business. And much of the "buzz" is about one of the fall's biggest releases, *The Scarlet Letter,* with Demi Moore playing a seventeenth-century Puritan.

Maybe you remember a novel called *The Scarlet Letter.* Written by Nathaniel Hawthorne, that was a story of love, guilt, and a society's merciless pursuit of even the best-intentioned sinners.

That was the old version. Good enough for Lillian Gish, if that's really your cup of chai, but strictly yesterday as far as

Hollywood is concerned. In Demi Moore's version, there are nude scenes and a happy ending. In the novel, everybody was miserable all the time. To figure out how you get a happy ending out of *The Scarlet Letter*, I guess you have to see the movie.

But just in case it sells, Hollywood is already trying to cash in, furiously rewriting the classics to exploit their megabuck crowd-pleasing potential for sex, violence, and happy endings. This is a direct appeal to the most desirable audience for the motion pictures these days: fourteen-year-old boys, who are often assigned the classics in school, but never finish reading them because they contain so many words, so few babes, and so few explosions.

I've caught the fever. So if anybody's interested, here are a couple of other ideas to put into development:

The Great Gatsby. A classic of the Jazz Age, remade as a vehicle for Sylvester Stallone. In this new version, self-made millionaire Jay Gats-bo receives word that his friend Nick Carraway is being held prisoner by enemy spies. Gats-bo arms himself to the teeth and singlehandedly rescues Nick. At one point, Gats-bo looks into the middle distance and mumbles the name "Daisy," but no one knows why, since of course there are no women or flowers anywhere in this picture. There's no other dialogue, either, but lots of really neat explosions.

Gone With the Wind. Sharon Stone, as Scarlett, sues Rhett Butler (Arnold Schwarzenegger) for spousal abuse. After a brief flirtation with her friend Melanie (Drew Barrymore), Scarlett will run off with Michael Douglas, the attorney who handles her case . . . repeatedly and in close-up. For background color, there's something about the Civil War, with lots of really neat explosions. Otherwise, fourteen-year-old boys might get bored.

For those boys, I offer a remake of a classic of American boyhood, *The Adventures of Tom Sawyer*. In my version, little Becky Thatcher (Alicia Silverstone) is kidnapped by a Caribbean drug kingpin, West-Injun Joe (Jeremy Irons). Tom Sawyer (Bruce Willis) arms himself to the teeth and singlehandedly rescues Becky, with lots of really neat explosions.

Years ago, people used to worry that the movies would keep Americans from reading enough. Now I worry that the people who don't read enough, are the people who make the movies.

REALLY USEFUL RATINGS
December 20, 1996

With all the debate about a television rating system these days, you'd think they'd have worked out all the angles already.

The idea is to have a system similar to that by which movies are rated, according either to the viewer's age or to the program's content, so that younger or more sensitive viewer's won't be able to watch. The so-called V-chip will block out any program depending on its rating.

But what will those ratings be, how will they be determined, and who will decide? One camp says TV should be rated according to the viewer's age, as movies are nowadays: "The following may not be suitable for children under the age of fifty-nine," for example. Others recommend a content-based system, advising viewers that programs may contain strong language, adult themes, or essays by Andy Rooney, any of which they may wish to avoid.

But this reporter has a few ideas of his own for a television rating system.

To begin with, I am tired of watching television shows that are unsuitable for viewers with an I.Q. over twelve. So I want a rating *D* for *Dumb*—and *DD* for *Dumber*. Shows that are Extremely Ridiculous should be labeled *E.R.*

If you don't want to watch Barney the Purple Dinosaur, shouldn't that show be rated *J.F.K.—Just For Kids*?

There are times I don't want to hear about a Certain Trial. So can we please have an *O.J.S.* rating? Not for *Orenthal James Simpson,* but for *Overplayed Judicial Story.*

P.S. would be the rating for game shows with players who are *Poor Sports.*

M.R.S. shows are guilty of *Mindless Racial Stereotyping.* *E.T.C.* would be the rating for *Extremely Talky Comedies.* During public television pledge breaks, we need a rating *B.L.T.* for *Bloody Long Telethon.*

I for one miss the old westerns, and want programs to be rated *I.C.C.* for *Insufficient Cowboy Content.*

There's a disturbing tendency of evening news programs to show other correspondents, instead of focusing exclusively on the anchor. That's why I want an *L.B.J.* rating, to cut down on *Long-winded Boring Journalists.*

Most of all, I want a "Me-Chip." It will block out everybody on the Evening News, except me.

After a while, I suppose you could rate and block out just about everything from your television set. Which leads to an important point. Nobody's rating system or V-chip is expected to improve the *quality* of television. Your best shot may be turning the set *O-F-F.*

Which is why I prepared these remarks for radio.

THE WEATHER OUTSIDE IS FRIGHTFUL
March 9, 1994

New York City has a reputation for short tempers and faulty manners, but the city may actually start to *deserve* that reputation if it snows one more time this year.

It's not that New Yorkers aren't willing to tough out the winter and help their neighbors make it through to spring. It's that there's been too much snow.

Call it "The Blizzard of Blahhs." New Yorkers are irritable and depressed and fed up. A friend of mine was actually spat on by a New Yorker the other day—because my friend had *not* nicked the paint job on the New Yorker's car. We're still not sure what the New Yorker would've done if my friend *had* nicked the paint.

Much of the rest of the country (about the same portion that thinks New Yorkers are rude) and most of the rest of the world can't figure out what New Yorkers are complaining about. In Minnesota, a run of blizzards such as the one New York has endured this winter is a walk in the park. You know that folks in Minnesota must think New Yorkers are wimps. They think, "Comes the next civil war, betcha Minnesota can lick New York."

Your reporter feels it's his duty to help others understand what's so rotten about snow in the Big Apple.

In the good old days (that is, any winter up until this year), snow in New York used to melt on contact with the pavement. We had wonderful snow scenes, fluffy white stuff swirling down from the skyscrapers and never, never getting in our way.

This winter, there's been so much cold and snow that the old snow seldom gets a chance to melt before a new snow falls.

This is bad enough, because space is at a premium in this city and there's really no room for extra snow. But consider, please, that in New York City, old snow is not white and fluffy. It's gray. It oozes. It's not pretty.

Snow is difficult to walk around in, and New Yorkers do a lot of walking. Walking is especially difficult when you're wearing heavy coats, heavy boots, thick underwear, thick gloves, and your nose is running and you can't reach the handkerchief in your pocket, six layers down . . . you get the picture.

Then there's the traffic. Half of New York drivers too often respond to a snowfall as if it were a bumper-car concession. The other half just stands completely still. The drivers driving too slowly irritate the drivers driving too quickly, and everybody hates the pedestrians.

You may or may not want to take these things into consideration the next time you talk to a New Yorker. But, for your own safety, please don't mention the word "bikini." Because we just can't take much more.

EL NIÑO AND THE BRILLIANT PEBBLES
March 4, 1992

Anybody who thinks El Niño was strictly a 1998 phenomenon has a short memory. Things were bad enough in 1992 that I was inspired to devise a solution.

We've been worried about a couple of things lately. Like the weather. Always a justifiable concern, but especially when it comes to El Niño, the bad weather that sweeps in from the Pacific with high temperatures and higher precipitation levels. Every few years it turns California into a wading pool. As I write this, it's just hit the Ventura area, and it's had too many Texans practicing the backstroke in their living rooms since Christmas. They call this thing El Niño, I guess, because nobody wants to be around when it grows up to be El Hombre.

Our other worry is the Strategic Defense Initiative, or S.D.I. Maybe you remember that S.D.I. was President Reagan's high-tech plan to thwart a nuclear attack by the Soviet Union. According to this plan, we'd have a screen or net of interceptors out in space that would zap the nukes before the nukes could hit us. Those interceptors were referred to as "brilliant pebbles."

Defenders of the plan say it's one of the things that brought the Soviet Union first to the bargaining table and then to its knees. Detractors call it "Star Wars." But every year the plan has gotten a little more money, and the project has proceeded.

Now that there's no more Soviet Union to worry about, we're worried about what will happen to all that research and development, and to the people who've been working so long.

Between El Niño and the Brilliant Pebbles, we've been so worried that we've had to divvy up the worry and take it in shifts. But then we realized we could worry about both at once, efficiently.

Why couldn't the Brilliant Pebbles be converted to another practical use? Like blasting El Niño out of the sky. The Pacific and the Southwest could be spared all the agony and multimillion-dollar expense of cyclical flooding, and all those space-defense technicians could keep their jobs.

And it wouldn't have to stop with El Niño. Getting too *little* rain? Just push a button and *zap*, the rain clouds would get shoved into position from someplace else—from Bangladesh to Ethiopia, for example. There'd be fewer benefit rock concerts, but we'd get used to that.

Eventually, we might even develop the technology so that everybody could have a portable, personal space-defense system. Call it "Pocket Pebbles." If it's raining on your parade, if a drunk is hassling you in a bar—*zap*. Maybe they could even work it so that the Pocket Pebbles could shield a person from disease, like cancer or the common cold or AIDS. Just zap those microbes. Wouldn't that be an inventive use of taxpayer money?

> *More recently, as the nuclear threat has resurfaced, S.D.I. is again being talked about. Like El Niño, we haven't heard the last of it yet.*

FOR WHICH WE WOULD BORROW A TITLE
FROM JAMES JOYCE
June 28, 1996

Like most reporters these days, I've been trying to figure out how to cover the news that First Lady Hillary Rodham Clinton has, allegedly, been having one-sided conversations with First Lady Eleanor Roosevelt. According to reports, Mrs. Clinton had writer's block while working on a book; with the guidance of a New Age counselor, she tried to imagine what advice Eleanor Roosevelt (who wrote a daily newspaper column) would give her.

Pretty simple. But New Age makes some people nervous, it gives rise to mockery, and it reminds some people of another recent bit of White House spiritualism, namely Nancy Reagan's use of astrologers to plan her husband's official business.

Giving a straightforward account of this story is pretty difficult. So I decided to ask the advice of a more experienced reporter.

I asked Edward R. Murrow.

The legendary CBS newsman died in 1965. But he pretty much invented electronic journalism, so whom else would you ask?

Ed and I haven't spoken in a while. Of course, during his lifetime I called him "Mister Murrow." But the older I get, the closer I get to death. Now Ed and I are on a first-name basis.

"Ed," I said, "how's afterlife?"

"Can't complain," said Ed. (Funny, ever since he died, Ed's voice has grown to sound remarkably like mine every time I talk to him.) Ed said, "Heaven is great. You'd love it. All the giants of CBS News are up here: Charles Collingwood, Eric Sevareid, Andy Rooney."

"Andy Rooney?" I said. "What's he doing there?"

Ed said, "You *know* Rooney's one of the greats, Dan: he's been telling you so for years."

"Yes," I said, "but he's not *dead*."

"Rooney never let a thing like that stand in his way," said Ed. "Besides, how else do you think he found the guts to interview Kevorkian?"

I tried to steer the conversation back to Mrs. Clinton. How is her talking to Eleanor Roosevelt any different from (for example) reports of Richard Nixon's talking to pictures on the wall of the White House?

"Hey, compared to some of the guys Nixon had to talk to, those paintings were a big improvement," said Ed. "Most of the dead don't mind when the living talk to us. Trouble is, how seldom the living listen.

"As for New Age philosophies," Ed went on, "I'm reminded of what John Lennon is always telling me: 'Whatever gets you through the night, is all right.' "

"But that's a terrible philosophy," I said. "What about drugs? Those may get you through the night, but they're not all right. What about cigarettes? They *killed* you!"

"I said I was dead, I didn't say I knew everything," Ed snapped. "Sometimes you've got to find the answers for yourself."

A wise man, that Murrow.

ACKNOWLEDGMENTS

No part of this book, or any part of my happiness, would be possible without the love and support of my wife, Jean, and our children: Robin and David, Danjack and Judy. You have taught me to see and hear, to feel and to live. You have guided and encouraged and sustained me. You are first among my blessings.

The inspiration for this book came from my weekly newspaper column, "Dan Rather Reporting," distributed by King Features. Writing the column has been a tremendous experience, and I am grateful to Joe D'Angelo, Larry Olsen, Ted Hannah, and everyone at King Features for making the process so easy and so fun. Day-to-day, my former editor, Maria Carmicino, was an unending source of encouragement and assistance. I know that her taste, diligence, and keen mind will be invaluable assets to her next employer, as they have been to King Features. I also extend my thanks and welcome to Chris Richcreek, who has proved a most worthy successor.

At William Morrow, I thank my editor, Zachary Schisgal, and all those who helped him.

But I must reserve my first gratitude for Frank Bennack, head of the Hearst Corporation. It was Frank who first proposed that I write the column. I don't know where he came up with the idea that I was capable of such a thing, but ever since I have worked my ass off trying to prove worthy of his confidence. Frank and his wife, Luella, have shown their friendship to me in so many ways that I will spend a lifetime paying off that happy debt.

Many of the other essays included in this book were originally broadcast on my daily radio program, *Dan Rather Re-*

porting. Although I write most of the pieces for that broadcast myself, radio is always a collaborative craft. I consider myself lucky to work with a number of excellent writers at CBS News who sometimes make their services available for my radio program. Moreover, they are unstintingly generous in lending their advice and assistance to my other writing projects. They inspire me to write better, and their work deserves to be published—every day. A few of their radio scripts are included in this collection. I would like to thank the following: Paul Fischer for permission to use his script, "Adoption"; Sakura Komiyama for permission to use her script, "The W.N.B.A."; and Greg Kandra for permission to use his scripts, "Oklahoma Explosion" and "Mantle." The extraordinary Elizabeth Dribben wrote the first draft of the script "Love Me Tender," which I then augmented with my personal reflections on Elvis Presley. I am also indebted to Frank Devine for writing "A Saint Who Knew What She Wanted," my newspaper column on Mother Teresa: because I was traveling to Mother Teresa's funeral, it wasn't possible for me to write a full draft of the column myself, but I would have deferred to Frank's superior knowledge of the subject in any case.

Some of the essays in this collection originally appeared (in one form or another) in the *Los Angeles Times, The Washington Post, London Evening Standard,* and the *New York Times.* Two others were destined for *National Review* and *Esquire* magazines. I am grateful to the editorial staffs of each of these distinguished publications, but perhaps most especially to Shelby Coffey III, formerly of the *Los Angeles Times,* and to William F. Buckley, Jr., for their extraordinary encouragement of my efforts.

Bill Madison worked as my in-house editor on all writing projects for a long while, including the time this book was conceived and put together. He also produced my radio program. I would be remiss if I didn't acknowledge his efforts in whipping my prose into shape—in nearly every essay I've written here. Moreover, his knowledge of the arts (especially popular music and old movies) and his sharp sense of humor contributed immeasurably to all the essays in the "Tributes" and "Lighter Side" chapters. Eric Wybenga worked long, hard, and well revising the book for this paperback edition.

Given the rigors of my schedule, it would be impossible for me to undertake the writing of any book without the assistance of a first-rate staff. Sakura Komiyama has provided me with outstanding support as the associate producer of my radio broadcast and the strong right arm of my office. Watching her grow as a journalist has been a privilege; enjoying the benefits of her already highly developed wisdom and maturity has been a blessing. Claire Fletcher's good cheer and good help have enhanced all our office projects.

I am grateful every day for the opportunity to work with the best in this business: I extend my thanks to Michael Jordan, Mel Karmazin, Les Moonves, Andrew Heyward, Jeff Fager, Al Ortiz, Susan Zirinsky, Marcy McGinnis, Linda Mason, Lane Venardos, Ted Savaglio, Michael Whitney, Michael Rosenbaum, Pat Shevlin, Janet Leissner, Wayne Nelson, George Osterkamp, Mary Mapes, Tom Phillips, Paul Fischer, Jerry Cipriano, Hugh Heckman, Toby Wertheim, Jim Moore, Debbie Margolis Rubin, Suzanne Meirowitz Nederlander, Terri Belli, Susan Shackman Adler, A. J. Warren, Eric Shapiro, Allen Alter, John Reade, Steve Jacobs, Kathryn Kent, Susan Martins Cipollaro, Amy Bennett, Cindy Pulis Dinan, Harvey Nagler, Mike Singletary, Kathleen Biggins, Erik Sorenson, and to every member of the team that creates the *CBS Evening News, 60 Minutes II, 48 Hours, Dan Rather Reporting,* the CBS News website, and all our broadcasts. I am proud to work with you, and prouder to call you my friends.

Wherever I go, I rely immeasurably on the counsel and friendship of Kim Akhtar and Duncan Macaulay, Bill and Carolyn Johnston, Eunice Martin, Mary Ann Quisenberry, Perry and Betsy Smith, Tom and Claire Bettag, Herb and Pat George Rowland, Richard and Carole Leibner, Red and Charline McCombs, Bill and Gloria Adler, Howard Stringer and Jennifer Patterson, Toby and Joel Bernstein, Charles and Mary Catherine Ball, Don and Gayle Canada, and Terri and Tim Vanackern, and David and Susan Buksbaum.

Special thanks must go to Eleanor Cunningham, Martin Anisman, Allen Zelon, Donna Dees, Ethel Goldstein, Sylvia Ellis, Don Richardson, Liz Carpenter, and Eve Bartlett.

Finally, I acknowledge the joyful inspiration of M. L., who has taught me the truth of St.-Exupéry's words, "What's essential is invisible to the eyes; we see only with our hearts."

INDEX